THE CHILDREN'S BOOK OF BRITAIN

Contents

Maps

THE CHILDREN'S BOOK OF BRITAIN

Jan Williamson and Susan Meredith

Illustrated by
Joseph McEwan,
Roger Mann and Bob Hersey

Maps by Swanston & Associates

Designed by Graham Round

Additional material by Mary Anne Evans and Robyn Gee

Some of the material in this book is taken from the Usborne Pocketbook title: *Junior Guide to Britain* by Mary Anne Evans and Robyn Gee.

First published in 1980 by Usborne Publishing Ltd, 20 Garrick Street, London WC2E 9BJ.

Printed in England by Purnell & Sons Ltd, Paulton (Bristol) & London.

The Story of Britain

Millions of years ago the shape of Britain was not at all like it is today. For much of the time Britain's land was under the sea and was not even in the same position on the globe.

This story tells you how Britain's rocks were made and how they rose and sank many times before they changed into the shape Britain is now.

About 4,600–3,800 million years ago

Scientists think the Earth started off as a ball of hot, liquid rock. As it cooled down, its surface hardened to a thin crust. The high parts formed blocks of land and the low parts were flooded by violent rainstorms and became seas.

About 3,000–600 million years ago

The oldest rocks in Britain are the remains of ancient volcanic islands. Millions of years later, rivers from nearby continents carried sand and mud into the sea over the rest of Britain. As they piled up, the bottom layers were pressed into new rock.

About 500–400 million years ago

Two ancient continents began to move together. They squeezed and folded the rocks between them and pushed them up from the sea to become land. There were many earthquakes and volcanoes. Mountains were made in Scotland, Wales and Northern Ireland.

About 2,500–400 million years ago

Life began in the sea. Simple plants started to grow and then worms, shellfish and bony fish gradually developed. About 400 million years ago the first animals crawled on to land.

The remains of plants and animals which lived millions of years ago are called fossils. You can see them in many sedimentary rocks, especially around the coast.

Different types of rock

Igneous rocks
Rocks made when hot, liquid rock from inside the Earth cools and hardens.

Granite may be white, grey or pink, but is usually speckled. It is hard and glittery.

Basalt is hard, black and heavy. It sometimes cools into six-sided columns.

Sedimentary rocks
Rocks made in layers under the sea from bits of other rock, sand, mud or shells.

Sandstone feels rough and sand rubs off it. You can sometimes see layers in it.

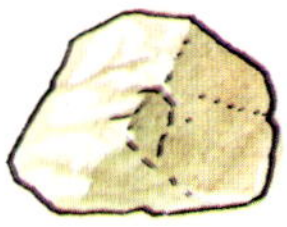

Chalk is soft and makes a white mark if you rub it on something hard.

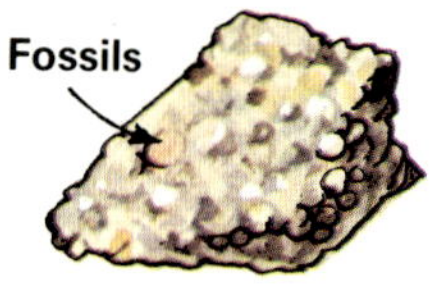

Limestone is grey, white or yellow. Look for layers and fossils.

Metamorphic rocks
Existing rocks which have been changed by being squeezed or heated inside the Earth.

Slate comes from mudstone. It is smooth and dark-grey and has layers which split apart.

Marble is made from limestone. It may be pure white or have swirly bands of colour.

Time chart

Millions of years ago	3000	570	500	435	395	345
What was happening in Britain	First rocks were made in Scotland Rocks appeared in Wales	Most of Britain was under sea Volcanoes in Wales and the Lake District Mountains were made in Scotland, Wales and Northern Ireland			Most of Britain was land Desert climate	Limestone formed in shallow sea Tropical swamps covered in coal forests
Geological name of period	Pre-Cambrian	Cambrian	Ordovician	Silurian	Devonian	Carboniferous

Britain's rocks are made

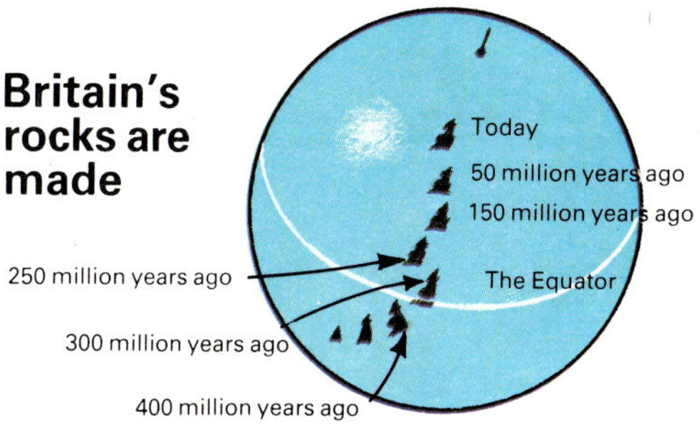

Over millions of years, earth movements have carried Britain across the globe. This journey has caused many changes in Britain's climate and has made a great difference to the rocks that have formed and the plants and animals that have lived.

About 400–350 million years ago

Britain's rocks were south of the Equator and part of a huge continent. The land was desert and a rock called old red sandstone formed. Today you can see old red sandstone in South Wales and parts of Scotland.

About 350–300 million years ago

Gradually the south of Britain sank under a warm, shallow sea, which was very clear and full of creatures such as sea lilies. Limestone rock began to form from the shells and skeletons of fish.

About 300–250 million years ago

Britain was on the Equator. The climate was hot and wet, and thick, tropical forests grew on the swampy ground. They were full of spiders, lizards, dragonflies and other creatures.

About 250–200 million years ago

There were new high mountains, mainly in southern Britain. The land was desert again and a new red sandstone was made. Salt and limestone formed in an inland sea which covered much of northern England.

About 200–150 million years ago

Dinosaurs and flying creatures called pterosaurs first appeared about 200 million years ago. Britain again began to disappear under the sea, leaving only islands of land. Clay rocks and limestones formed in the sea.

About 150–100 million years ago

As the land rose again, the south of England became part of a huge, muddy swamp. Herds of iguanodon dinosaurs grazed in the swamp, feeding on rushes and horsetails. There were many salt lakes and lagoons.

About 100–50 million years ago

Britain disappeared completely under a huge, shallow sea, which was full of creatures. Thick layers of chalk rock formed from their shells and skeletons. Today you can see chalk on the south coast of England.

About 50–25 million years ago

Mammals spread after the dinosaurs died out (about 65 million years ago). The Atlantic Ocean was opening up to the north west of Britain and the last large area of new rocks was made around London and Hampshire.

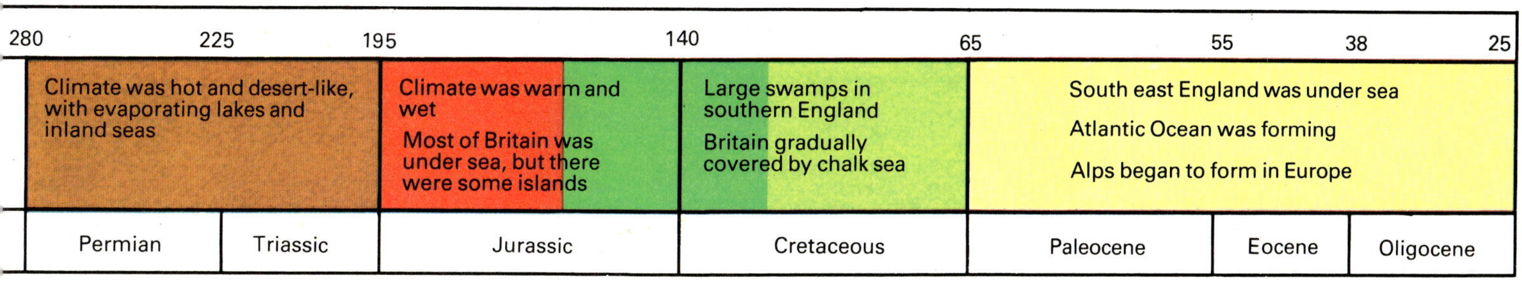

The Story of Britain

Almost all of Britain's rocks have been land for the last 25 million years, but they have changed a great deal during that time to make the landscape we see today.

As soon as new rocks are pushed up from the sea to become land, they start to be worn down again. Wind, water and ice break off small pieces of the rock and carry them away.

In many parts of Britain, rocks on the surface have been completely worn away over the ages to show older rocks underneath and entire mountains have been lowered to plains.

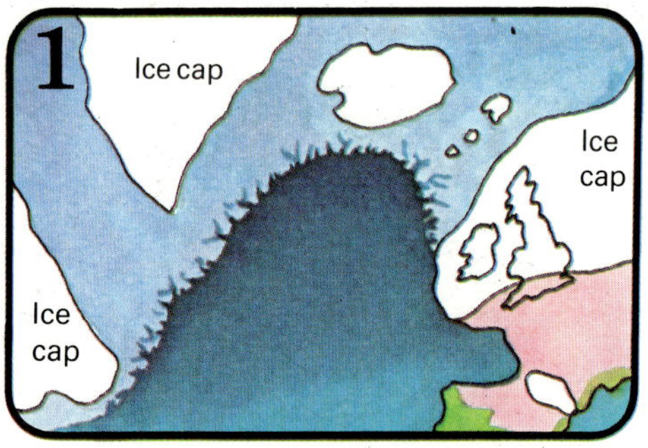

About 2½ million years ago the world began to get colder as ice caps spread from the North and South Poles. Several times much of Britain was covered by ice, though in between the ice ages it was often warmer than it is today. At present we may be in a warm period before the next ice age.

As it got colder, the snow built up, especially on high land. After many winters the lower layers were pressed into ice.

The mountains of Scotland, Wales and the Lake District were all shaped by ice. Glaciers scooped out deep, steep-sided valleys and hollows. Many of the hollows are now lakes. Ice sheets smoothed and rounded the landscape, but any peaks that stuck through the ice are sharp and jagged.

When the glaciers melted, they dropped rocks and mud that they had picked up on their journey. In places these have made a hummocky landscape.

Some huge boulders, called "erratics", were carried a long way before being dropped. This one in Yorkshire may have come from Norway.

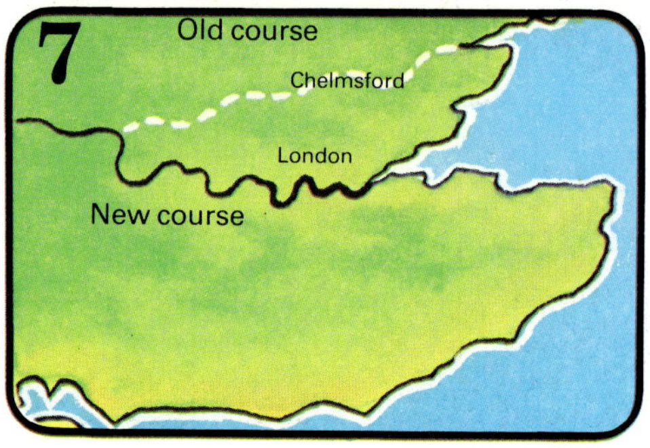

Many rivers had to change course during the ice ages. The River Thames used to flow into the sea in East Anglia but as ice sheets moved south, they blocked its route and it was forced to flow east along the front of the ice. After the ice melted the river kept its new course.

Rivers

In a wet climate like Britain has now, rivers are important in wearing down rocks. Rivers pick up stones, sand and mud where they are flowing fast in the hills and then drop them on the plains and as they enter the sea. The stones, sand and mud then start forming new rocks in the sea.

Soft rock wears away more easily than hard rock, so river valleys usually follow lines of soft rocks, or old cracks and weak places in the rock. Mountains like Snowdon and Ben Nevis are the highest in Britain because they are made of hard rock and so take longer to wear away.

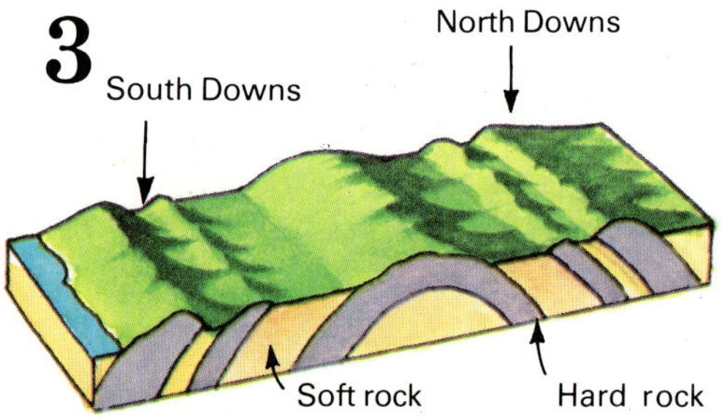

The speed at which different rocks wear away makes a pattern of hills and valleys. In eastern and southern England the hard rocks are sandstone, limestone and chalk and they have made hills called "escarpments". The soft clay rock has made broad valleys between the escarpments.

Time chart

Years ago	25,000,000	7,000,000	2,000,000 1,000,000
What was happening in Britain	Atlantic Ocean got wider South east England was slowly folded while the Alps were made in Europe		Britain's newest rocks were made only 2 million years ago in East Anglia World climate became colder. Ice sheets advanced and retreated across Britain several times. In cold times, mammoths and woolly rhinos lived. In warm times (between ice sheets) elephants and hippos lived.
Geological name of period	Miocene	Pliocene	Pleistocene

The ice became glaciers and the weight of more snow falling on top forced them to move downhill along valleys.

3

When many glaciers join together, they make an ice sheet. At one time ice sheets stretched as far south as London.

The glaciers got so big that they filled up their valleys. Then they spilled over to join up with each other, covering all the land between them except the highest peaks.

8

Southern England was never covered by ice, but it had an arctic climate. The soil was permanently frozen and rivers from the ice sheet further north flowed over the surface, cutting valleys in the rocks. You can still see these valleys, although many of them no longer have rivers.

9

At the end of the ice ages Britain was joined to Europe. Then, when the ice melted, it ran into the sea and the sea level rose. Water flooded the Channel and Britain became an island off the coast of Europe. There are old tree stumps around Britain's coast from forests which used to be land.

10

The rising sea drowned the lowest parts of valleys, making many inlets and estuaries. The long inlets in south Wales and south west England are drowned river valleys called "rias". The deep inlets on the west coast of Scotland, called "fiords", were once filled by glaciers.

Britain now and in the future

1

When the great weight of ice melted from northern Britain at the end of the ice ages, the land slowly rose. Parts of Scotland are still rising today and there are old beaches now far above the seashore. In contrast, the south and east of Britain are slowly sinking.

2

Around the coast waves wear away rocks. Soft rocks often form bays and hard rocks make headlands. In East Anglia the rocks are so soft that about 150,000 square metres of land are washed away every year. The entire town of Dunwich has disappeared over the cliffs in the last 600 years.

3

In 80 million years time scientists think Britain might look like this. New mountains have been pushed up in the Irish Sea and the Channel, so that mainland Britain is joined to Ireland and Europe. There are volcanoes in Ireland, high mountains in south west England and sea over eastern Britain.

500,000	10,000	8,000	5,000
The first people reached Britain. They were hunters and lived in caves in the Mendip Hills	The last ice sheets melted in Scotland	English Channel, Irish Channel and North Sea were drowned by melting ice, making Britain an island	More groups of people came to Britain from across the sea
Holocene			

The Story of Britain

The previous four pages explain how Britain's landscape has been shaped by natural forces over the past 3,000 million years. Here you can see how it has been changed by people over the last 5,000 years.

As the climate began to get warmer at the end of the last ice age, thick forest grew all over Britain. In order to work the land successfully, some of the early farmers started to clear it away. People continued clearing forest for several centuries and now it has almost all disappeared.

3000BC–AD43

The first farmers in Britain did not alter the landscape much. They had simple stone tools which were not strong enough to clear much forest and they had to farm the more open hill tops. The Celts had stronger iron tools. They cleared land and farmed small, square fields.

AD43–AD410

The first towns and roads in Britain were built by Roman invaders. Many of our towns are on the sites of Roman ones and you can see Roman remains.

AD450–AD1066

The Anglo-Saxons ignored the Roman towns and roads and cleared more forest to build villages. They farmed their land in big open fields, divided into strips. The first churches were built, but they were mostly in wood so few have survived. Many present day villages date from Anglo-Saxon times.

AD1066–AD1450

By the time the Normans conquered Britain in 1066, some villages had grown into towns, although the population of Britain was still very small. Towns continued to grow during the Middle Ages and you can still see the remains of many castles, churches and monasteries that were built at this time. In spite of the development of towns, most people still lived in villages, farming strips of land for the lord of the manor.

Time chart

Date	3000BC	1900BC	700BC	AD43	AD410
Important people	First farmers in Britain arrived from Europe	More farmers came from the Netherlands and North Germany	Celts arrived from Europe	Romans conquered Britain	Angles, Saxons and Jutes came from North Germany and Denmark Scots went from Ireland to Scotland. Native Picts died out Vikings attacked from Scandinavia
Name of period or people	Stone Age	Bronze Age	Iron Age	Roman	Dark Ages

AD1450–AD1700

By 1700 almost all the thick forest in Britain had been cleared away to be used for house building, ship building and fuel.

AD1700–AD1780

Gradually the countryside became more like it is today. The big open fields were divided into smaller ones by hedges and ditches. New crops, new machinery and better breeds of cattle were introduced. Farms became more efficient, but many people lost their land and had to move to the towns.

AD1750–AD1830

Canals were built to transport heavy goods like coal and iron, and roads improved after the turnpike system of charging tolls was introduced.

AD1780–AD1900

Britain became the first heavily industrialized nation in the world. Big towns grew up, especially near the coalfields, which provided power for factories. Railways became the main form of transport. Today you can see disused mills with tall chimneys and rows of workers' terraced houses.

AD1900–Today

Towns have got so big that they often join up with one another to form "conurbations". New industries have developed using electricity for power, which means they no longer have to be sited near supplies of coal. Motorways have replaced railways as the main means of transport. Much of the countryside has disappeared and the population of Britain is now about 56 million – nearly 30 times larger than it was a thousand years ago.

AD1066	AD1485	AD1603	AD1714	AD1837	AD1901
Normans conquered Britain Henry II	Henry VIII Elizabeth I	Charles I Queen Anne	George I George II George III George IV	Queen Victoria	
Middle Ages	Tudor	Stuart	Georgian Age	Victorian	20th Century

Rock map

This map shows you some of the main types of rock which make up the land of Britain. The key gives you their geological name and you can tell from the time chart on pages 4–6 how many millions of years ago the different rocks were made.

The pictures round the edges of the map show you just a few examples of the types of landscape you can see in Britain today.

The oldest rock in Britain is in the Western Isles. It is a grey, metamorphic rock, called gneiss. Ancient rock like this lies hidden under newer rocks in other parts of Britain.

These ancient hills have flat tops because they have been worn down by rivers. They may once have been as high as Everest.

Great cracks, or faults, sometimes appear in the landscape as a result of earth movements. This is the Great Glen fault, which cuts right across Scotland.

Edinburgh Castle stands on top of the core of an old volcano. The softer rock surrounding the core was worn away long ago by ice.

Waterfalls are made where a river crosses from hard to soft rock. The soft rock wears away more quickly, making a step in the river bed. This is High Force, one of Britain's highest waterfalls.

At Malham Cove, in Yorkshire, you can see this strange limestone pavement. It is made by rain water seeping into cracks. The water dissolves the rock and widens the cracks.

Much of the Midlands is pasture land, but in places you can still see ridge and furrow marks under the grass from when the land was ploughed in the Middle Ages.

The hollow of Red Tarn, on Helvellyn, was once the source of a glacier and filled with ice. The sharp ridge on the left of the picture, which is called Striding Edge, was cut by ice.

Belfast Lough was drowned by the sea at the end of the last ice age. It is very deep and sheltered, which makes it a good place for shipbuilding.

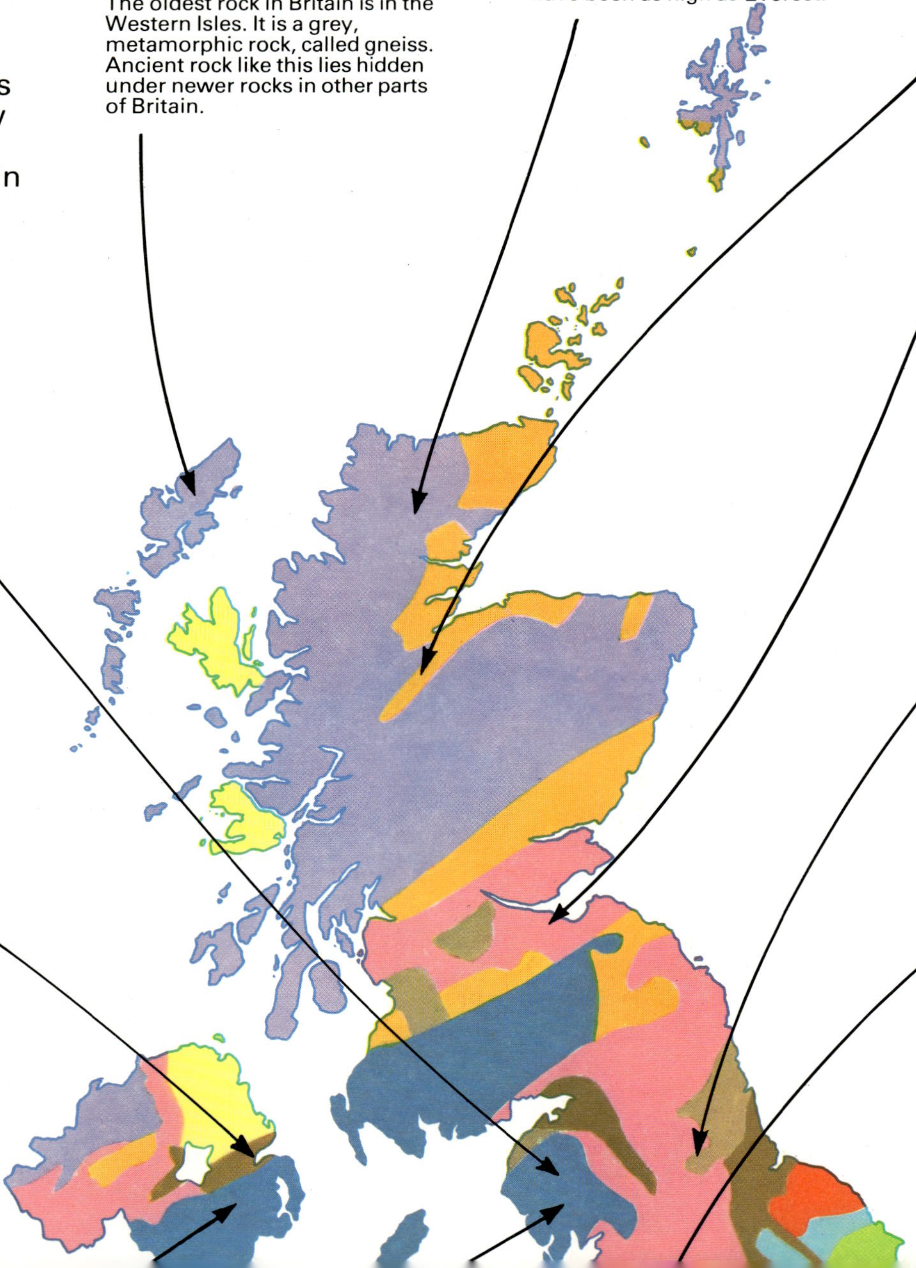

This hummocky type of landscape is sometimes called a "basket of eggs". It was made by a melting ice sheet, which dropped lumps of clay and then smoothed them over.

This is loose rock called "scree" on the Old Man of Coniston. When water freezes in the cracks in rock, it expands and breaks up the rock into smaller pieces.

The Llanberis valley has steep straight sides and the typical U-shape of a valley cut by the ice of a glacier.

Most of Britain's coal lies underground and has to be mined. You can usually tell a coal mine by the tower and wheel which work the lift.

This is Hay Tor on Dartmoor. It is made of granite which was pushed up, when it was molten, into the surrounding rocks. It gradually came to the surface as the top rocks wore away.

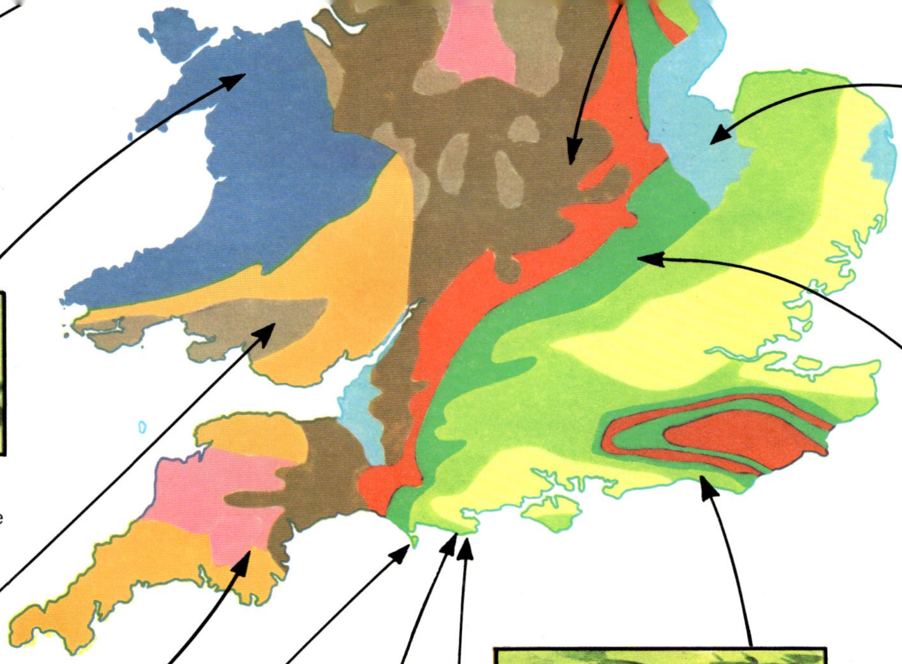

In some places, the sea builds new land by dropping sand and pebbles to make ridges. At Chesil Beach a pebble ridge has joined Portland Island to the mainland.

These pillars of rock off the Dorset coast are stacks. They may once have been arches whose roofs collapsed.

The sea has worn through the limestone headland near Lulworth Cove to make this arch, which is called Durdle Door.

The South Downs are a line of chalk hills with a steep slope on one side and a gentle one on the other. There are few streams as water soaks into the chalk.

The Fens were a marshy part of the Wash until much of the area was drained. Windmills pumped water into rivers and ditches and the Fens now have the most fertile farmland in Britain.

Clay is used to make bricks. At these brick works in Bedford the pits from which the clay has been dug are now filled with water.

Key to map colours

Rock types	Geological name
Igneous and metamorphic	Pre-Cambrian
Old sedimentary and volcanic	Cambrian, Ordovician and Silurian
Old red sandstone	Devonian
Limestone and millstone grit	Carboniferous
Coal	
New red sandstone and limestone	Permian and Triassic
Limestone and sandstone	Jurassic
Clay	Jurassic and Cretaceous
Chalk	Cretaceous
Sands, clays and volcanic	Paleocene, Eocene and Oligocene
Silt and mud	Most recent

Prehistoric and Roman Britain

Prehistoric Britain

You can see many prehistoric remains in Britain. Prehistory is the story of man before written records began. It divides into three main periods: the Stone Age (3000 to 1900BC), the Bronze Age (1900 to 700BC) and the Iron Age (700BC to AD43).

Monolith (also called a Menhir). Single standing stone. Probably put up as religious monument.

Trilithon. Two upright stones supporting a third. Usually part of a stone circle.

Hill figures have been cut into chalk hillsides in some places. They may have been gods or emblems of tribes. Not all of them are prehistoric.

Hill fort. Hill fortified by ditches and earth banks. Built in the Iron Age, mainly in south of England. This is Maiden Castle in Dorset.

Stone circles. Prehistoric people built stone circles called "henges". They probably used them for measuring the movements of the sun and stars and for religious ceremonies.

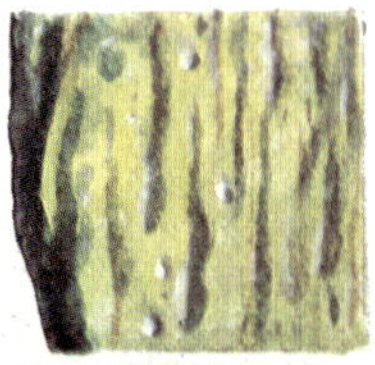

Tool marks. Simple stone hammers were used to shape the stones. You can still see the marks they made.

Stonehenge

One of the most famous prehistoric monuments in Europe. Built over 4000 years ago on Salisbury Plain in Wiltshire. The largest stones reach about 7m above ground and 3m below.

On 21 June, the longest day, the sun rises over the heelstone and shines into the centre of the circle.

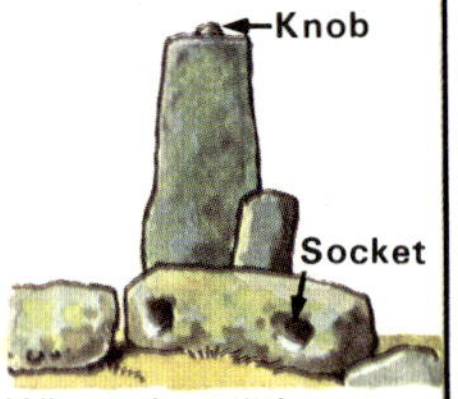

Where the trilithons have fallen down you can see the **knobs and sockets** which held them together.

Mounds and tombs

If you see a grassy mound like this one it may be a Stone Age tomb called a **long barrow.**

Inside long barrows are passages and chambers where people were buried.

Stone rings, like this, may have been entrances to burial mounds. They are quite rare.

A round grassy mound might be a Bronze Age tomb called a **round barrow.**

A barrow where the earth has worn away, leaving bare stones, is called a **dolmen.**

Silbury Hill in Wiltshire is a **man-made hill** built by prehistoric people. We do not know why they made it.

In the Orkney Islands there are the remains of a **Stone Age village** called Skara Brae.

You can see the remains of huts and courtyards at Chysauster, an **Iron Age village** in Cornwall.

Brochs. Tall, round towers built as fortresses in Iron Age. Found in Scotland.

Reconstructed farm

At Butser in Hampshire a research team has built an Iron Age settlement and is using Iron Age methods to farm the land.

Looking for flints

Prehistoric men made tools out of a hard stone called flint. Look for flint chips and tools if you are near prehistoric remains. They look like this.

Things to look for in museums

This page shows some things you might see in Prehistoric and Roman collections in museums. Many towns and archaeological sites have museums displaying objects found nearby.

Bronze Age clay beaker found in burial mound. These have patterns of lines scratched on them.

Iron Age helmet. Shields and swords from this period have also been found.

Roman glass is very delicate. Jugs like these were made by blowing hot glass into moulds.

Scenes from Roman life. This is a reconstruction of a mosaic craftsman's workshop.

Armour and weapons of Roman soldiers. This model is at Grosvenor Museum, Chester.

Roman wall painting. Specially good ones are on display at the St Albans Roman Museum.

Roman vase showing gladiators fighting. Many show scenes from Roman life.

Roman coins often have pictures of emperors' heads on them.

Sculpture and statues made by the people living in Roman Britain (left) were much rougher and less life-like than the ones brought from Rome (right).

How to find ancient sites

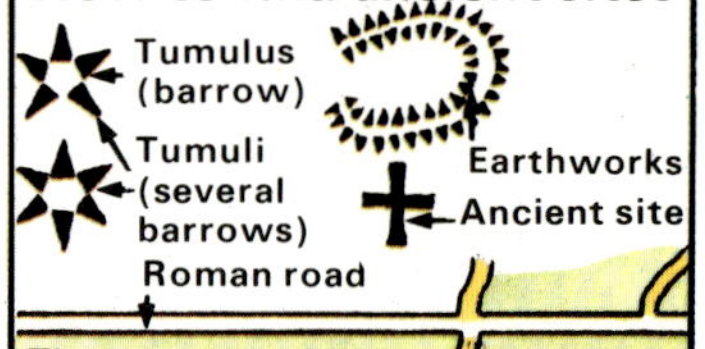

The above symbols and words are used on Ordnance Survey maps to mark the places where you can find Prehistoric and Roman remains.

Roman Britain

The Romans first invaded Britain in AD43. By AD84 they had completed their conquest, although they never really controlled Scotland or the furthest parts of Wales. They ruled for about 350 years and you can still see the remains of many things that they built. This section shows you what to look out for. The map marks the main Roman towns, roads, villas and fortifications.

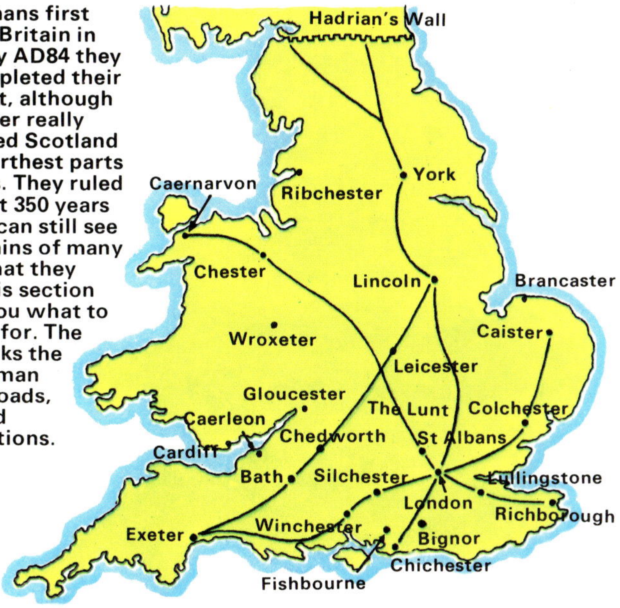

Villas

Roman villas were large country houses. There are several places in England where you can visit the remains of one. This is a model of the villa at Fishbourne as it probably looked in Roman times.

Mosaic. Pattern made of small pieces of coloured glass, stone or marble. Often used to decorate floors.

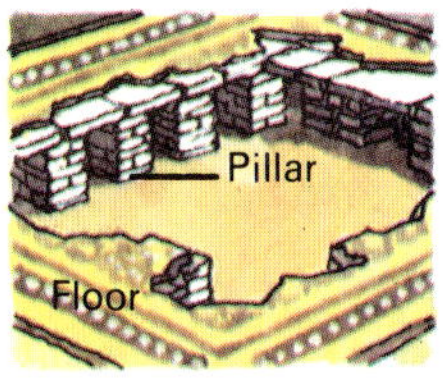

Hypocaust. Part of Roman central heating system. Space under floor heated by hot air from furnace.

Shrine. Many houses had underground shrines or temples where people prayed to their gods.

Towns

In a few places the remains of a Roman **forum** (market place) have been uncovered.

You can often spot a **Roman wall** by the line of red tiles running through it.

In some old towns you can see **Roman arches** and bits of their walls.

This is part of the **Roman Baths** at Bath in Avon, which were built above hot springs. They were rebuilt and used long after Roman times.

Look out for archaeologists at work excavating ancient sites. If they dig deep enough they sometimes find Roman remains.

Hadrian's Wall

The Emperor Hadrian built a wall, 122km long, to protect Roman Britain against the warlike tribes who lived in Scotland. You can still see where the wall went.

There was a **milecastle** every $1\frac{1}{2}$km along the wall, each defended by 50 soldiers.

There were 16 **forts** built at intervals along Hadrian's Wall and seven on the south side to give it extra strength. These are the reconstructed defences of the fort at Chesterholm.

Granary at Housesteads. Pillars raised the floor so that air could circulate and keep the corn dry.

Theatres

You can still see one or two Roman **amphitheatres** (circular arenas surrounded by seats), like this one at Caerleon in Wales. Here people watched shows, chariot races and gladiator fights. They also built semicircular **theatres.** The foundations of the theatre at St Albans are shown above.

Temple at Carrawburgh. Remains of temple where the Roman god Mithras was worshipped before the Romans became Christians.

Dover lighthouse

This is the only Roman lighthouse in Britain still standing. It was originally over $26\frac{1}{2}$m high and fires were kept burning inside it all night. It is one of two which were built at Dover. The other one has now gone.

Roads

Foundation Stones of Roman road. Roman cities were linked by long straight roads.

Very straight modern roads (not motorways) are often based on the foundations of **Roman roads.**

Milestones marked every Roman mile (1,000 paces) along the roads.

The Lunt Roman Fort

This is a reconstructed Roman fort near Coventry. Mock battles are staged here by a society called the Ermine Street Guard.

Saxon shore forts

Part of the shore fort at Richborough one of several built to defend the south and east coast against Saxon raiders.

Castles

There are hundreds of castles in Britain, varying from early motte and bailey types to huge palaces. This section is about older castles, most of which are in ruins.

If you are going to visit a lot of castles, it might be worth buying a season ticket. You can get these at many sites, or by post from the Department of the Environment, 25 Savile Row, London W1. Tel: (01) 734 6010.

If you want to remember the castles you visit, it is a good idea to buy a guidebook at the entrance. If you take a notebook and pencil along with you, you can draw the things you see and make notes as you walk round (see opposite page for ideas). If you have a camera, take a few photographs too and afterwards you can put together a proper record of your visit.

Most English castles were built between 1050 and 1600, when kings and lords needed somewhere to defend their families against enemies. Many were altered and added to as designs changed.

Windsor Castle is one of the homes of the Queen and royal family and is the largest inhabited castle in Europe. It was founded by William the Conqueror, added to over the years and largely rebuilt in the 1820s. You can go inside the Chapel and State Apartments.

Things to spot at castles

Here are some things to try and spot if you visit a castle. Most of them are things that were useful for keeping out enemies, whose main weapons were bows and arrows, catapults, battering rams and siege towers.

Moat. Deep water-filled ditch surrounding a castle to deter enemies. Some have now been drained.

Drawbridge. Bridge for crossing moat that could be raised or lowered from inside the castle.

Portcullis. Strong wooden and iron grating for blocking gateway. Set in grooves so it can slide up and down.

Arrow slit. Hole in wall through which defenders could fire arrows without becoming targets for their attackers.

Gun-loop. After the invention of cannons, holes through which to fire them were often cut below arrow slits.

Murder holes. Holes in roof of a passage through which things could be dropped on to enemies below.

Machicolations. Holes in parapets or battlements through which stones and weapons were thrown.

Wall-walks between towers gave soldiers a good view of the countryside on all sides when they were on guard.

Spiral staircases, which wind around a central pillar inside towers, connect the separate storeys of a castle.

Fireplace. In ruined castles you often see fireplaces high up on the walls. This shows where floors used to be.

Beam holes. Sometimes in ruined castles you can see the holes where the beams that held up the ceilings fitted.

Early castles were built on a mound called a **motte** with a courtyard called a **bailey** at the bottom.

Most early stone castles had a **square keep** (main building) like this one at Rochester Castle.

Round keeps, like this, were built because they were easier to defend than square ones.

Later castles were strengthened by outer or curtain walls. These are called **concentric castles.** Edward I built eight of them in Wales.

Henry VIII built a chain of **rose-shaped castles** along the coast to protect England from invasion. This is Deal Castle.

Most castles were built of stone but in the last years of castle building a few **brick castles** were built.

In the 1800s it was fashionable to build houses that looked like castles. These are called **Gothic castles.**

Many **Scottish castles** are really fortified houses with the main living rooms on the upper floors.

Sham castles, like Mow Cop castle in Cheshire were built to provide romantic views rather than to be lived in.

Jousting

In the summer, at some castles, people dress up as knights and have mock battles. To find out where jousts are being held, contact the Jousting Association, Chilham Castle, Kent.

Armour and weapons

Look out for these on display at castles.

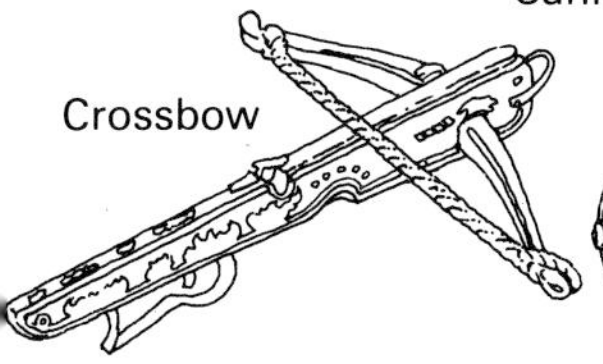

Crossbow

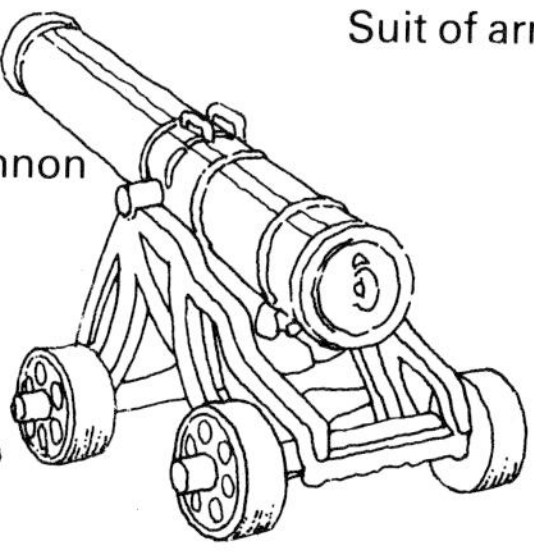

Cannon

Suit of armour

Here are some examples of siege weapons that were used to attack castles.

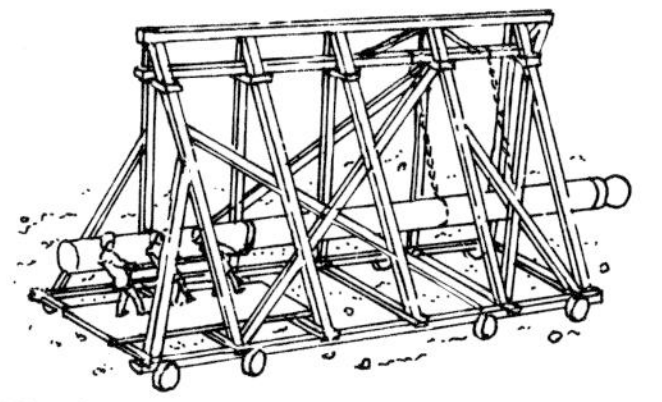

The **battering ram** – a tree trunk with an iron cap on one end – was swung on ropes against doors or walls.

Wooden **siege towers** were pushed up to the walls so the attackers could fight directly with the castle soldiers.

Dungeons

In some castles you can visit the **dungeons**. They are usually underground and very dark and damp.

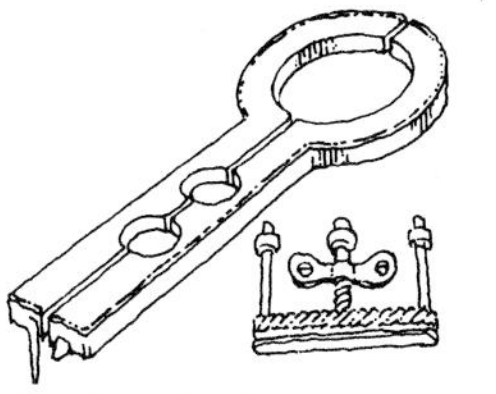

Torture instruments, like these thumb screws and iron collar, were used to punish prisoners.

Sometimes you can see the **names and dates** of prisoners scratched on the walls of dungeons.

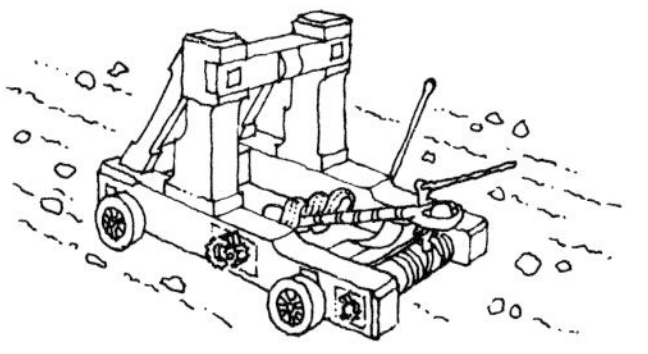

The **mangonel** was a catapult used to throw stones and other heavy missiles.

Attackers often dug **tunnels** under the foundations of a tower. When the props of the tunnel were set alight, the tunnel collapsed and brought the tower down with it.

Visiting a castle

History. Find out who built the castle and when. Who is the owner today? Have any famous people been associated with it? There may be an effigy of the owner in the local church or a portrait in the local museum. Finally, try to find out why the castle fell into disuse.

Site. Look at the castle's position. Is it built on a hill, in an old town, by a river, on the coast, in open country? The site will give you a clue as to why the castle was built in the first place and what it was defending.

Defence. Walk round the castle and see how good the defences were. Is there a moat? Could the stream feeding it be easily diverted? Is there any high ground nearby from which a stone-throwing machine could pound the walls?

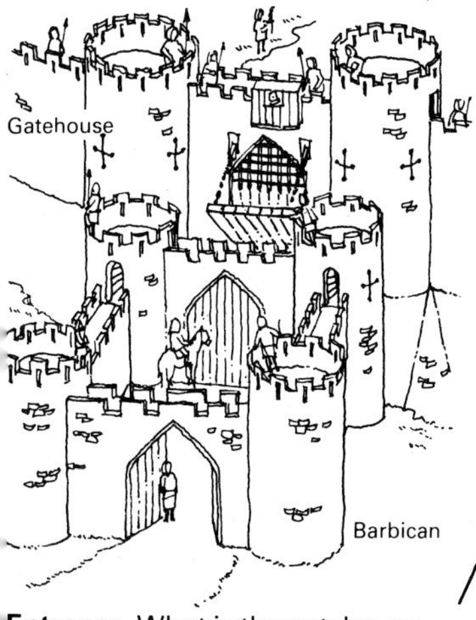

Entrance. What is the gatehouse like? Is there a barbican? A drawbridge? A portcullis? If not, are there any clues to tell you they were once there? Are there grooves in the gateway that held a portcullis, or machinery for a drawbridge?

Framlingham Castle, Suffolk

HISTORY – Begun in 1100. Improved over the centuries by the Howard family, dukes of Norfolk, who were given the castle in 1397. There are tombs of the dukes in the local church. Mary Tudor was living here when she was proclaimed queen. In 1636 the castle was given to Pembroke College, Cambridge, and most internal buildings were pulled down.

SITE – On a large mound. Built to protect the surrounding countryside.

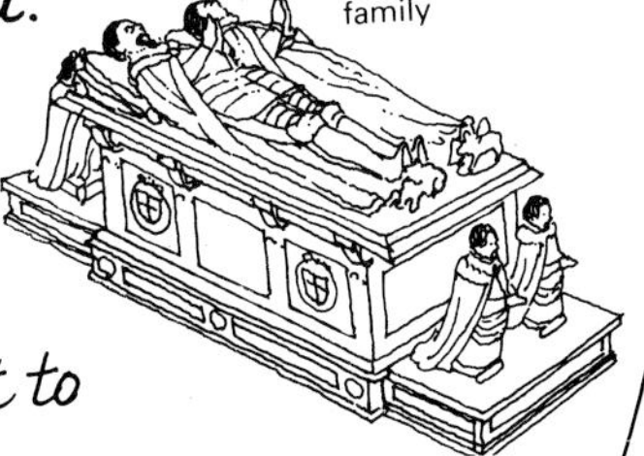

Tomb of Howard family

DEFENCE – Moat (now dry) was originally fed by River Ore. Difficult to divert the stream.

ENTRANCE – Large gatehouse. Original drawbridge over moat now gone.

CURTAIN WALL – High curtain wall with 13 towers, mostly square. Spiral stairs. Many fireplaces and latrines. Good field of fire from wall-walk.

INTERNAL BUILDINGS – No keep. Only buildings left inside are a poor-house, built about 1640, and a brick great hall.

Brick chimneys

CHANGES – Tudor brick chimneys added in reign of Henry VII.

WEAPONS – No weapons on show, but tombs in church show Howards in armour.

Curtain wall. Walk round the wall and see how good a field of fire there is on to the surrounding countryside. How easy is it to get to the wall-walks from the curtain wall? How many wall towers are there? Are any of them named? Are they square or round? Do they have spiral stairs? Do the rooms in them have fireplaces?

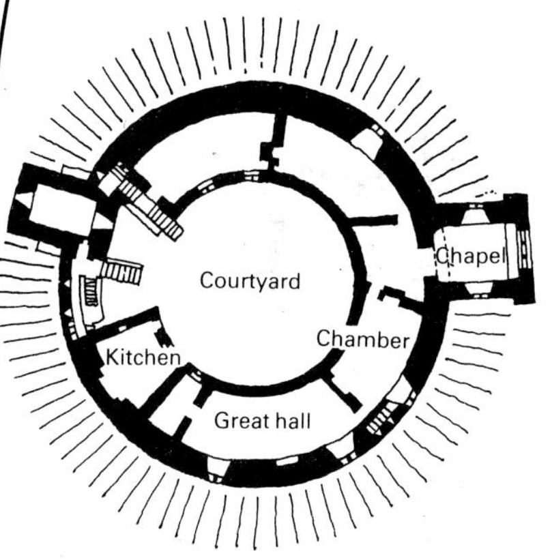

Plan of a keep

Internal buildings. Is there a keep? What shape is it? Look at a plan if you can. How many rooms were there? Did it have a hall, chapel or kitchen? Look up: can you tell how many floors there were by beam holes, fireplaces or windows?

Changes. Look for any later changes to the castle. Have the buildings been heightened? Have any comforts been added, like brick chimneys? Have windows replaced arrow slits?

Weapons. Note down any weapons that are on display. In the local church there may be a brass of a knight in armour you can rub (see page 17).

Churches

Looking round churches can be fun if you have things to look out for. On the next pages, you will find some clues to the age of a church, a selection of things to spot in them and some information about different types of churches. Before you go into a church to look round it, make sure there is not a service in progress. There are usually several services on Sundays.

Cathedrals

A **cathedral** is a large church which contains the throne of a bishop or archbishop. There are 56 in Britain, many of which are famous for their architecture.

The **West Front** is often elaborately decorated with stone carvings.

The clergymen who run the cathedral have meetings in the **chapter house.**

See if you can find the **bishop's throne** or *cathedra* (Greek word for seat).

Cathedrals that were once monastery churches have **cloisters.** These are covered arcades round a square where the monks could walk and meditate.

Some churches were once part of a monastery or nunnery and the old name of abbey is still used for a few, like Bath Abbey. Others are now called cathedrals.

Ruined abbeys

There are many ruined abbeys (once monasteries and nunneries) in Britain. Most of them were destroyed by Henry VIII between 1536 and 1540, when he broke away from the Catholic Church.

If you visit a **ruined abbey,** see if you can find the part where the monks slept (the dormitory) and where they ate (the refectory). There is usually a plan of how it used to look on a notice board or in a guide book.

Churches

There are over 19,000 parish churches in Britain. In many towns and villages, the church is the oldest building. For centuries, it was the centre of the community and so it can tell you a lot about local history.

Look out for yew trees in the churchyard. They may be even older than the church. Also look for a weathervane on the steeple. The most common is a cock, the symbol of St Peter.

Chapels

Large churches often have several chapels in them. The **lady chapel** is usually behind the main altar.

Chantry chapels, often with railings round them, were paid for by people who wanted prayers said for them.

Regimental chapels are for the special use of an army regiment. They usually have the regiment's flag in them.

Sometimes chapels were built in remote areas because the main church was too far away. These are called **chapels of ease.**

Some independent religious groups, like the Methodists, call their places of worship **chapels.**

Organs

Organs have been used in churches for hundreds of years, but for a long time only important churches had them. Until the middle of the last century smaller churches used a band of musicians playing recorders, fiddles and cellos.

The organ is usually in a loft or gallery. Look for the long pipes. Each one plays a different note when air is let in.

The organist has keyboards and a panel of stops to work with his hands, and pedals for his feet.

Clues to the age of a church

You can tell from the style in which a church is built roughly how old it is, although some churches have been restored and added to in a mixture of styles. Here are the names of the main styles used in the Middle Ages, when most British churches were built.

Norman		1066-1189
Early English	Gothic	1189-1307
Decorated	Gothic	1307-1327
Perpendicular	Gothic	1327-1509

To date a church, try matching its doors, windows and overall shape to the pictures below. You will also see Gothic features in Victorian churches (1837-1901). These are often built of brick, so they are fairly easy to spot.

Doors

Towers and spires

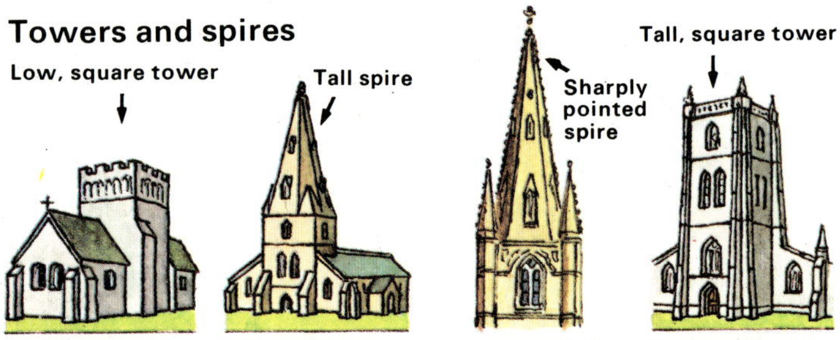

Windows

Things to Spot in Churches

Gargoyle. Stone spout to keep water from gutter clear of wall. Usually carved in the shape of an ugly head.

Flying buttresses. Arches on the outside of a building which act as props to hold the walls in place.

Sanctuary door knocker. In the Middle Ages, anyone who touched it could claim sanctuary and be safe from arrest.

Hammer-beam roof. Type of wooden roof that has no cross beams to support it. Often beautifully carved.

Fan vaulting. Stone roof with ribs branching out like the sticks of a fan.

Roof boss. Ornament placed where the ceiling ribs meet. Often carved and painted like this one.

Box pew. Pew with high wooden sides. You get in and out through a door.

Poppy-head bench-end. Decoration on the top of a bench-end. There are many different poppy-head designs.

Misericord. Hinged seat in choir stall for resting on during long services. The underside is often carved.

Rose window. Round window usually filled with tracery (patterns made by thin strips of stone).

Squint. Opening in an inside wall which gives a view of the high altar, when it was hidden by a rood screen.

Rood screen. Carved wood or stone screen which separates the altar from the congregation.

Crypt. Underground room beneath most cathedrals and large churches. People were sometimes buried here.

Eagle lectern. Wood or brass eagle with outstretched wings for holding an open Bible.

Carved font cover. Often so heavy it has to be lifted by chains (The font holds water for Christenings.)

Pulpit with sounding board to reflect the preacher's voice towards the congregation.

Pulpit with hour glass to tell preachers how long they have been talking for. Often, only the iron bracket is left.

Chained Bible. You can sometimes see Bibles that were chained for safe-keeping when books were very valuable.

Tombs

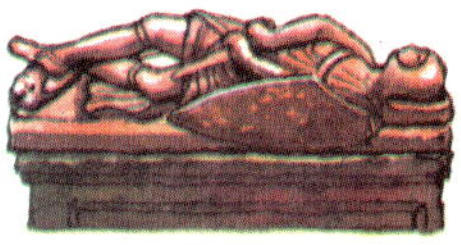

If the figure on the tomb is a knight with **crossed legs** he was probably a crusader.

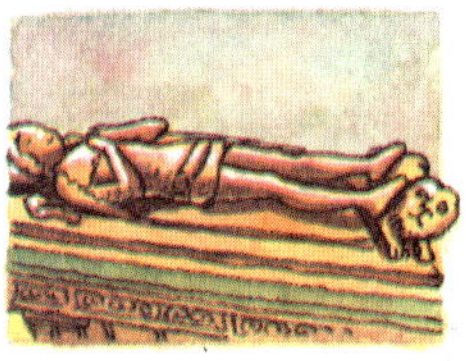

If the figure on a tomb rests his **feet on a lion** it means he died at war, if his feet **rest on a dog** he died at home.

The kneeling figures on this tomb are called **weepers.** They represent mourning members of the dead person's family.

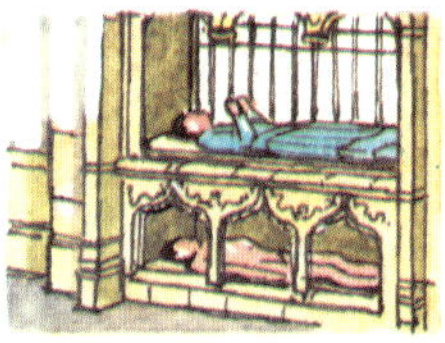

Sometimes tombs of very holy people show a **skeleton beneath the main figure** to make people think about death.

From the 1540s onwards figures in casual attitudes became popular. A favourite position was **leaning on one elbow.**

Some early tombs have **niches for receiving pilgrims' offerings** cut into the sides.

Pictures in churches

In the days when most people could not read and write, painted, carved and glass pictures in churches helped people to learn Bible stories. You will often see **stained glass windows showing Bible scenes.** This one shows Adam and Eve with the serpent in the Garden of Eden.

In some churches, there are **pictures carved round the tops of pillars.** This one from Wells Cathedral shows a farmer hitting a fruit thief over the head.

Wallpaintings have survived in only a few churches. The Last Judgement, showing Jesus judging people's souls at the end of the world, is a common subject.

Church bells

Most churches have a set of bells hung in the tower. Each one plays a different note and bellringers ring them in changing sequences by pulling on long ropes. Look for the **bell ropes** tied up against the wall.

Brasses

You will often see brass plates, engraved with pictures of people, fixed to the walls and floors of churches. They were put up as memorials to dead people. You can take rubbings from them, but you must ask permission from the vicar first and usually pay a small fee. There are also several brass-rubbing centres where you can rub copies of brasses.

The pictures on **brasses** are usually of important people, like bishops, lords, ladies, knights and merchants. The oldest ones date from the 1200s.

To do a brass-rubbing you need paper, tape and heelball wax. First tape the paper down over the brass, then rub the wax over the paper until the complete image has appeared on the paper.

Roman numerals in dates

Dates on old buildings are often given in Roman numbers, like this: MDCCXLIII (1743). Here is how to work them out. I = 1, V = 5; X = 10, L = 50, C = 100, D = 500, M = 1000. Where a number comes before a number larger than itself, subtract e.g. IV = 4 (5 – 1), IX = 9 (10 – 1). Otherwise add the numbers together e.g. VII = 7 (5 + 1 + 1).

Great Houses

England is famous for its great country houses. Some are still lived in by the descendants of the noble families who built them, others belong to organizations which keep them in good repair. Most are open to the public at certain times of the year. The houses on this page show how styles of architecture changed over the years. When you visit a great house, see if you can tell which style it belongs to.

Oxburgh Hall, Norfolk, is a fortified manor house built in the 1480s. Early manor houses often have a moat and strong gatehouse like this.

Blenheim Palace, Oxfordshire, (built 1705–1722) is in the Classical style, which was copied from Ancient Greece and Rome. This style has lots of columns.

Harewood House, Yorkshire (built 1759–1771) has a central building with "wings" attached at either end, like most large houses built in the Georgian period (1714–1830).

This is Longleat House in Wiltshire, one of the fine country houses built in the Elizabethan age (1558–1603). Many of these are built in the shape of an "E"

In the Jacobean period (1603–1625, when James I was king) brick was a popular building material. This is Hatfield House, Hertfordshire, which was built between 1607 and 1611.

The Royal Pavilion in Brighton is in a style of its own. The outside looks Indian, the inside Chinese. It was built for the Prince Regent, who later became George IV.

In Victorian times (1837–1901) many houses, like Knebworth House in Hertfordshire, were rebuilt in a style called Gothic, which was first used in the Middle Ages.

Things to spot in great houses

Minstrels' gallery. Balcony in Great Hall used by musicians who played at feasts.

Painted ceiling. These often illustrate myths or famous stories.

Secret door. Blends with wall so it is hidden when closed.

Family crests

Many families have their own coat-of-arms, something like this, which is passed down through the generations.

Metal stamps for making **wax seals** on documents often have the crest from the coat-of-arms on them.

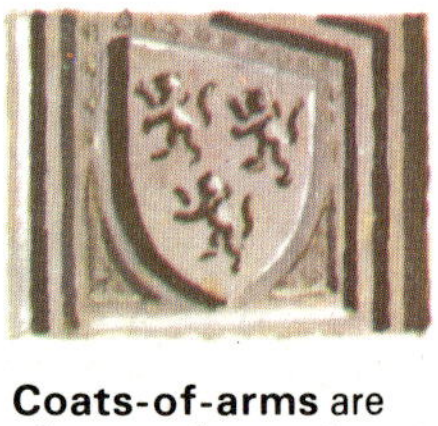

Coats-of-arms are often used as decoration, specially over doorways and fireplaces.

Linenfold panelling. Design in wood pannelling which looks like draped cloth.

Fire screen. Used by ladies to shield their faces from the heat of the fire.

Silent companions. Painted wooden figures, usually by fires, said to keep ladies company.

Portraits

See if you can spot any family likenesses between the people in the paintings in the house. They are often ancestors of the family who owns the house.

Ghosts

If you visit an old house ask if it is supposed to be haunted. This is the ghost of Catherine Howard, the fifth wife of Henry VIII, who is said to haunt Hampton Court.

Four-poster bed. The curtains were drawn at night to give privacy and keep out draughts.

Basin and jug. Before houses had bathrooms, maids brought water for washing to the bedrooms.

Bellrope. When this was pulled a bell rang in the servants' part of the house.

Gardens

Knot Garden. Low box hedges divide the flower beds into elaborate patterns.

Topiary. Shrubs clipped into ornamental shapes, often of birds or animals.

Sundial. A shadow cast by the sun falls on a surface marked with hours and shows you the time.

Warming pan. These were filled with hot coals and used for warming and airing beds.

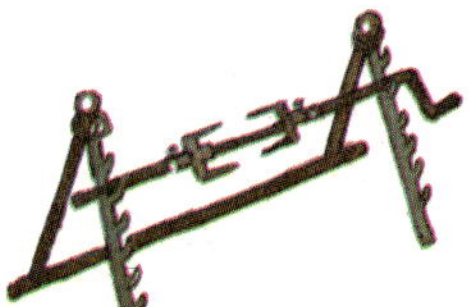

Spit for roasting meat over a fire. A boy turned the handle so meat cooked on all sides.

Mirror with candles. The light was reflected by the mirror and so made the room brighter.

Temple. At one time it was fashionable to build mock temples as garden ornaments.

Maze. Complicated network of paths with high hedges on either side. There is only one way to the centre and back again so it is easy to get lost in them.

Some country houses are still as they were built originally, others have been altered over the years. The furniture is often in different styles too. Here are a few clues to help you tell the age of the things you see.

Tudor and Jacobean houses 1480s–1625

The great hall was the showplace, used for entertaining important guests. The floor was made of wood, stone, or black and white marble squares. Look for wood panelling on the walls, or tapestries.

The long gallery ran the whole length of the house. Ladies walked here when it was too cold or wet to go out, and children were taught their lessons. Notice the wood panelling and the small-paned "mullioned" windows.

The Classical style 1625–1714

The Classical style was introduced into England by architects and designers like Inigo Jones. Arches over doorways (called "pediments") and columns were used to give an elegant, well-balanced look.

By this time there were many more rooms and they were smaller. One of the most important was the dining room. Thin wooden panels called wainscotting covered the walls, and the walls and doors matched perfectly. Ceilings were plastered or painted and floors carpeted.

The Georgian Age 1714–1830

Most large country houses were built in the reign of the king Georges, again in the grand Classical style. The main room was the great hall where guests were received.

Robert Adam was a famous architect who designed whole rooms to match, in soft, pastel colours. He often used the same patterns in his ceilings and carpets, and even in the furniture.

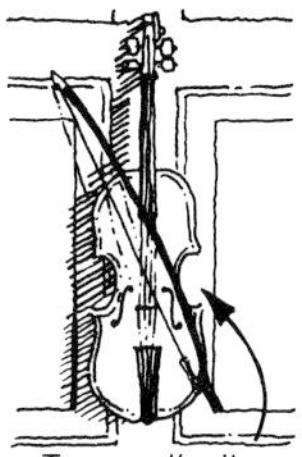

Trompe l'oeil

The main staircase was very grand and wide. Sometimes the paintings on the walls look so life-like you believe the people and objects in them are really there. This is called *trompe l'oeil* painting, which is French for "deceives the eye".

Many houses were built so you passed straight from one room into another, even from bedroom to bedroom. You can often look down the whole length of the house.

Houses were heated by coal, which burned in marble fireplaces. The mantlepieces were often decorated with Roman-style vases, which Josiah Wedgwood made popular.

It was in the 18th century that tea-drinking became a popular British habit. Elaborate tea tables, caddies and pots were designed and porcelain tea cups were used.

Furniture to look out for

Tudor furniture is usually made of oak. It is heavy and solid, and has different designs carved on it.

Tudor Jacobean

Spot the difference between a Tudor and a Jacobean design.

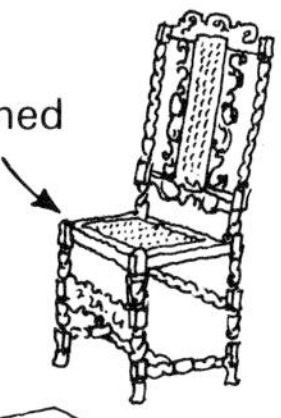

Cane-bottomed chair

17th century furniture looks less heavy and is often made of walnut. Look out for these things.

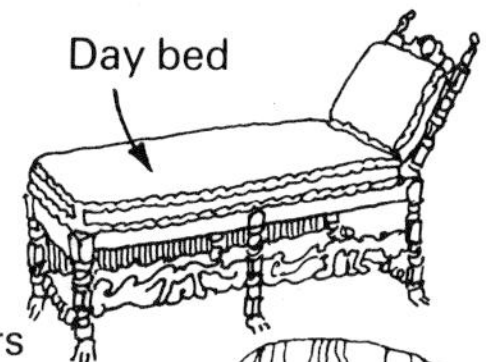

Day bed

Chest of drawers

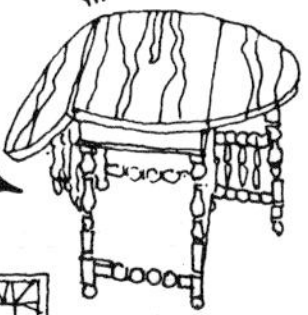

Gateleg table

In the 18th century mahogany was used as well as walnut, and lots of furniture was veneered. This means that a thin sheet of beautiful wood was glued on to furniture made of cheaper wood. Patterns were made by glueing veneers together.

Veneer

Veneered cabinet

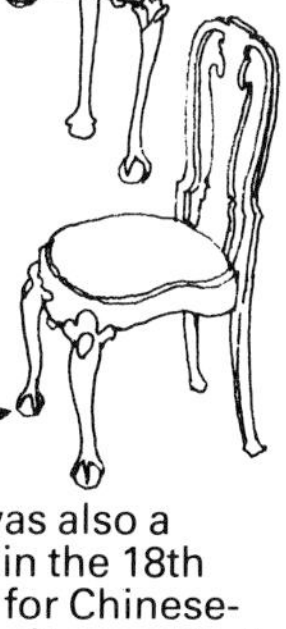

Claw and ball foot

Queen Anne style furniture is easy to recognize by the curved shape of its "cabriole" legs. These often have claw and ball feet.

There was also a fashion in the 18th century for Chinese-style furniture, called "chinoiserie". Sometimes people had whole rooms decorated in this exotic style.

Towards the end of the 18th century, pieces of furniture became smaller and more delicate, and legs straight and tapering.

Towns

Edinburgh, the capital city of Scotland, is built on hills and crags. This is Princes Street, the main shopping street.

York has many streets which were built in the Middle Ages and have changed little since then. This one is in the area called the "Shambles".

Bath. Famous for its hot springs since Roman times. Much of it, including the Royal Crescent (above), was built in the 1700s.

Stratford-upon-Avon. William Shakespeare was born here. This is the Royal Shakespeare Theatre where his plays are performed.

Chester also has buildings from the Middle Ages. The "Rows", shown above, are open passages along the first floor of the houses, with shops leading off them.

Warwick grew up around a castle. This 14th century building is Lord Leicester's Hospital, built for poor people to live in.

Oxford. Famous for its university. The round building is the Sheldonian Theatre, used for university ceremonies and concerts.

Cambridge. Also famous for its university. Here you can see people punting on the river Cam, in front of King's College.

Things to look for

Towns used to be surrounded by **city walls** for protection. In some old towns you can still see them.

City walls had **gateways** in them. These were the only way in and out of the town and were closed at night.

In the Middle Ages many town houses were built with **overhanging storeys.** This made the streets very dark.

Before tarmac and concrete, road surfaces were made of stones. Small irregular stones are called **cobbles.**

Gas lamps, made from ornate iron, were used to light the streets. Many have now been converted to electricity.

An **old-fashioned street name** often tells you what was sold in that street.

A **porte-cochère** (coach door) is an archway to the court-yard of an inn or house, wide enough for a coach and horses.

Old-fashioned shop signs showed symbols of the shopkeepers' trades. **Three gold balls** is the sign for a pawnbroker's shop.

Victorian pillar boxes have VR on them, which stands for *Victoria Regina* (Latin for queen). They are often six-sided.

Many town parks have a **bandstand,** where a band plays in summer. The fashion for these started in the early 1800s.

Local residents sometimes decorate their area with **wall-paintings,** on the sides of buildings.

Walls with stubs of iron on top once had railings. The iron was cut down and used to make weapons in World War II.

Things to spot on buildings

Mason's mark. When a stonemason worked on a building he often signed it with his mark and the date.

Link snuffer. Used to put out flaming torches, which were carried to light the way before there were street lamps.

Fire insurance sign. Showed which company had insured a building because each one had its own fire brigade.

Twisted chimney stack. Built in Tudor times (1485–1603). They are made of brick and are often patterned.

Blocked up windows. From 1695 to 1851 there was a tax on windows so people blocked them up to avoid paying it.

Wall anchors help to hold outside walls straight. They are attached to beams or rods inside the building.

Local museums

Objects, like these Saxon brooches, give clues about the people who lived in the area a long time ago.

Some museums, like the Castle Museum in York, have made reconstructions of parts of the town as they used to be. You can walk through cobbled streets, lit by gas lamps and go into old shops.

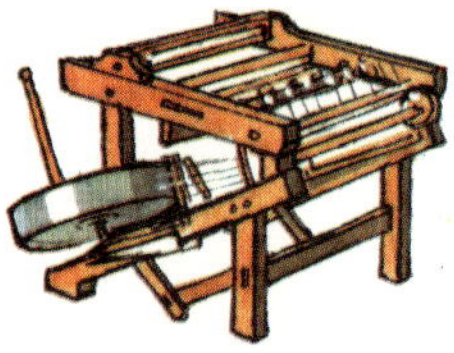

Tools and machinery, like this spinning jenny used for making cotton, tell you about working life in the past.

The houses of famous people are sometimes turned into museums. This is the room where Shakespeare was born.

Some museums produce leaflets which tell you where to go to spot historic things around town.

Different types of towns

When you go to a town, see if you can find out why it grew up in the first place, and when? Most towns started off as small villages centuries ago, but they usually developed where they did for a reason. Here are just a few examples of different types of towns with ideas of what to look for in them.

Cathedral cities

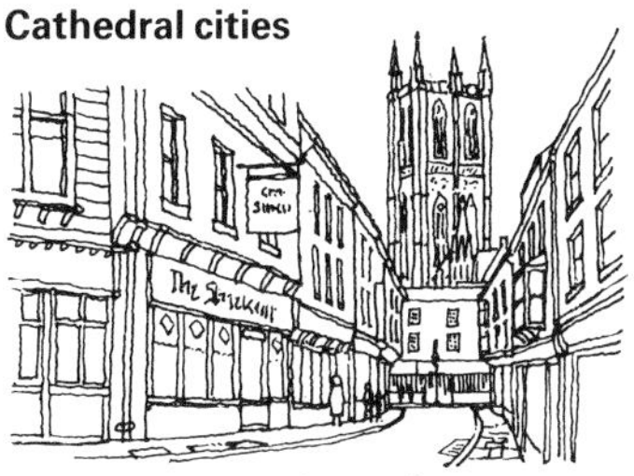

Butchery Lane, Canterbury

Any town with a cathedral is called a city. See if you can find out when the cathedral was built. Many medieval towns grew up round cathedrals and the oldest, most interesting streets to explore are the narrow, winding ones near the cathedral. Look for dates and inscriptions on the old buildings. Canterbury, Durham and Salisbury are examples of cathedral cities.

Market towns

Marlborough high street

Some towns had markets as early as the Middle Ages. Clues to look for are a very wide main street or a large square. Look out too for an old market hall or a market cross. See if you can find out what sort of market the town used to have originally and whether it is still held.

Norwich market square

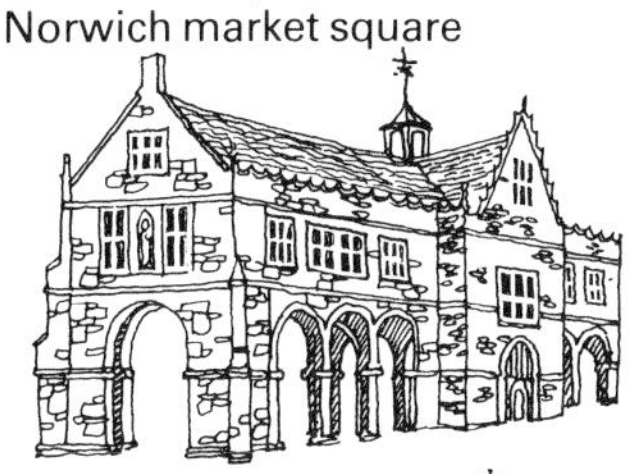

A market hall

Market crosses with shelves for displaying goods

Wool towns

Most of these are in the Cotswolds and Suffolk, which were important centres for the early wool trade. Wealthy wool merchants built many of the old buildings in towns like Chipping Campden and Lavenham, sometimes even the churches. See if you can find the merchants' tombs. Look out too for houses with lots of windows upstairs. These were to give weavers light to work by. You may also see inns called "The Fleece" or "The Woolpack".

Lavenham

Brass of a wool merchant

County towns

These are where county councils have their headquarters. You can often tell a county town by its name. Leicester is the county town of Leicestershire and Ayr of Ayrshire. Take care, though, as this does not always work – Derbyshire's county town is not Derby, but Matlock.

Spas

Tunbridge Wells

Towns like Cheltenham Spa, Leamington Spa and Tunbridge Wells became fashionable because they had healing mineral waters. Look for elegant 18th century buildings, housing the baths and pump rooms, and see if you can spot "The Spa Hotel", "The Royal Pavilion" or "The Spring Gardens". There may still be somewhere in the town where you can taste the waters.

The Pittville Pump Room, Cheltenham

Industrial towns

In the 19th century, large industrial towns grew up around factories, mainly in the north of England, the Midlands, South Wales and Central Scotland. Many of them have now been modernized, but you will still see smoke-blackened buildings, old mills with tall chimneys, and streets of small terraced houses. The finest building in an industrial town was often the town hall or the railway station.

Mill at Hebden Bridge

Row of terraced houses

Manchester town hall

New towns

Modern new towns, like Milton Keynes, Runcorn and Livingston, are now being built in Britain to avoid overcrowding in other places. They are carefully planned in advance with factories, offices, shops and schools. Look out for very unusual buildings or sculptures.

The swimming pool at East Kilbride

Place names

Place names can tell you about a town's origins. The end or beginning of the name is usually the bit to look for. Here are some examples which go back to very early times.

Roman		
-caster	fortified place	Lancaster
-cester	fortified place	Gloucester
-chester	fortified place	Chichester
Anglo-Saxon		
-borough	fortified place	Wellingborough
-burgh	fortified place	Edinburgh
-bury	fortified place	Shrewsbury
-combe	valley	Ilfracombe
-ham	small village	Chatham
-ing	the clan of	Reading
-ley	meadow	Chorley
-stow(e)	meeting place, holy place	Felixstowe
-ton	village	Kingston
Scandinavian		
-by	village	Derby
-thorpe	small village	Scunthorpe
-toft	farmstead	Lowestoft

Scottish		
Aber-	river-mouth	Aberdeen
-an	small	Ardrossan
Dun-	fort	Dundee
Inver-	river-mouth	Inverurie
Kil-	church	Kilmarnock
Kirk-	church	Kirkcudbright
-ness	promontory	Inverness
Welsh		
Aber-	river-mouth	Aberystwyth
Caer-	fort	Caernarfon
Car-	fort	Cardiff
Llan-	church	Llandudno
Pont-	bridge	Pontypridd
Irish		
-agh	field	Armagh
Bally-	path	Ballymena
-derry	oak grove	Londonderry
Don-	hill-fort	Donaghadee
Down-	hill-fort	Downpatrick
Dun-	hill-fort	Dungannon

Longest place name in Britain: Llanfairpwllgwyngyllgogerychwyrndrobwllllantysiliogogogoch. This is a town in Wales, often abbreviated to Llanfair P.G.

Street names

Street names will give you lots of clues to a town's history. Here are a few of the obvious ones, but see if you can spot any that have more unusual meanings.

Baker Lane
Castle Hill
Wood Street
Oakdale Road
Victoria Crescent
Bishop's Avenue

Town facts

Smallest town in Britain:
Caerwys, Clwyd, Wales, 800 people

Ten largest towns in Britain:

Greater London	6,970,000 people
Birmingham	1,050,000 people
Glasgow	832,000 people
Leeds	735,000 people
Sheffield	547,000 people
Liverpool	537,000 people
Manchester	492,000 people
Edinburgh	464,000 people
Bradford	462,000 people
Bristol	410,000 people

Villages

Villages grew up in different places for different reasons. You can often tell from its shape why a particular village started where it did. Here are some examples. See if you can spot villages like these.

Some villages are grouped round a **village green**, which is common land belonging to the whole village. There is sometimes a duck pond in the middle. Finchingfield in Essex is a good example of this type of village.

Many villages are grouped **around a crossroads** because, in the old days, this was a good place to trade.

Villages on the coast are usually grouped **around a harbour or bay** instead of a green. This is Mevagissey, a fishing village on the coast of Cornwall.

Often a village lies in the **bend of a river.** Originally the river would have supplied water and been a good defence against raiders.

Some villages grew up **along a busy highway,** often a trade route. These are long and narrow. Broadway in Worcestershire is like this.

Sometimes villages grew up **around a castle or monastery.** At Dunster, in Somerset, the castle is at the top of the hill and the village is at the bottom.

In mountainous areas, like Wales, villages grew up **on the side of the valleys.** Many Welsh villages look like this.

Things to spot

Here are some things to look out for when you visit a village. Many villages grew up in the Middle Ages and some of the things you see will date from that time. Look out for dates on old buildings.

Manor House or Hall. Usually the largest house in the village. The Lord of the Manor used to live here.

Pub. Might be several hundred years old. Look out for a date on the sign or carved over the door.

Old school building. Usually about 100 years old. Sometimes has separate entrances for boys and girls.

Almshouses. These were built by rich men as homes for old people. They are often long low buildings or rows of cottages, and have tall chimneys.

The churchyard is often the oldest part of the village. Look at the names and dates on the tombstones. See which is the **earliest date** you can find. You might find several graves with the same family name on them.

A churchyard gate with a roof is called a **lych-gate.** "Lych" is the old English word for dead body.

Crosses

Celtic cross. Often not cross-shaped, but has cross carved on. Very old. Put up by early Christians.

Market cross. Might be called a Butter Cross or Wool Cross, according to what was usually sold there.

War memorial. This is a reminder of people who died in war. See which war it commemorates.

Punishments in the Middle Ages

Stocks. People had to sit with their feet locked through the holes.

Whipping post. People were tied to this post and then whipped.

Ducking stool. Women who nagged were put on one of these and ducked in the pond.

Pillory. The lawbreaker stood on the platform and his head and hands went through the holes.

Lock-up. A small, solid building with no windows which was used as an overnight prison.

Other village things

Pound. Stray animals were caught and put in here. Their owners had to pay to get them back.

Dovecote. People used to eat doves (pigeons). They kept the birds in stone huts like this.

Tethering post. This was where people tied up their horses.

Horse trough. Stone basin filled by rain for animals to drink from.

Pump. Water was often drawn up from underground by pump before villages had mains water supply.

Well. A bucket on a rope reaching down to the underground water. To raise it, you wind the handle.

Looking round a village

Little Bidlington in the Marsh is an imaginary village, but it shows you the sorts of things you might discover in a real one. Try finding out the answers to some of these questions next time you go to a country place.

1 Why did the village grow up in the first place? Its shape or position may be a clue. (See the top of the page opposite.)

2 How old is the village? Try looking for dates on the graves in the churchyard, on tombs inside the church and on buildings like the pub.

3 What are the buildings made of? Are most of them in the same material and is this local to the area? Notice the shape of the roofs. (See page 24.)

4 What kinds of buildings are there? Is there a manor house? An almshouse? A school? When was the church built and in what style? (See page 16.)

5 Are any names particularly common in the village? Again, look at gravestones, or signs over shops. Some families may have been there for generations.

6 If there is a pub, where did it get its name? If it is called "The Travellers' Rest", for instance, can you find out where the travellers were going?

7 Are there any particularly unusual things in the village with interesting stories attached to them? (See opposite page for some examples.)

8 What special traditions are there? Things like village fêtes and carnivals often stem from old customs and beliefs.

9 Did the villagers practise any special crafts in the past and have any been revived? Look out for a craft centre in places like an old mill or barn.

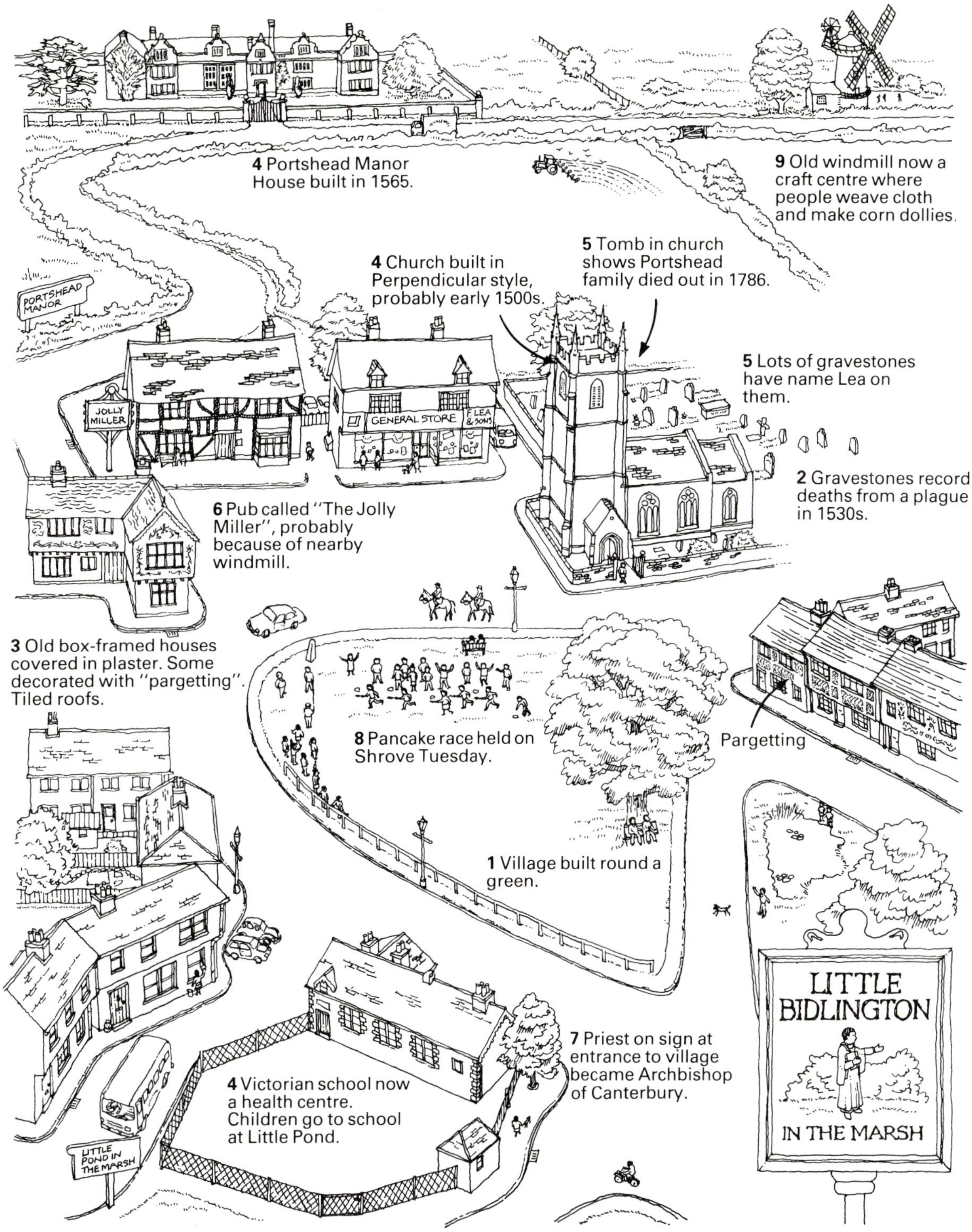

Pub signs

As you travel about, it is fun to spot pub signs. There are thousands of different names for pubs, but here are some of the main types. When you spot a sign, see if you can tell which of these types it is.

A bush was the original trade sign for a drinking house. "The Grapes" and "The Chequers" are also early pub names.

Some pubs started as inns that provided food, drink and lodging for pilgrims, merchants and other travellers.

Sometimes pubs take their names from famous events. This one is called after Nelson's great victory at sea.

Some pubs are called after famous people. Dick Turpin was a well-known highwayman.

In country districts, you often see signs connected with farming or local trades and crafts.

Some pub names have a religious meaning. "The Star" gets its name from the Star of Bethlehem.

Many pubs used the name of the local lord and painted his coat-of-arms and family motto on the sign.

There are lots of pubs named in honour of the kings and queens of England.

You will probably see lots of pubs with the names of birds, animals and fishes.

Look out for pubs with names taken from a sport. These are not very common.

There are lots of pubs with joke signs. Here the "load of mischief" is the man's wife.

Houses and Country Buildings

Houses

Here are some old houses to spot. In the past, people usually built houses out of local materials and many areas developed their own particular style of building.

Rough stone walls and slate roof. You will see a lot of cottages like this in Scotland, Wales, Ireland and Cornwall.

Cob and thatch. Walls made of a mixture of clay, gravel and straw, called cob. Roof of straw or reeds.

Cruck-framed. Crucks are curved wooden beams which reach from the ground to the roof and support the house.

Box-framed. These houses are made of a wooden frame, painted black, which is filled in with plaster, usually painted white.

Limestone. This golden coloured stone is found mainly in the area called the Cotswolds. The stones are usually smooth and neat.

Flint. This is a very hard, steely grey stone, found in chalky areas. Flint houses often have brick frames round the doors and windows.

Tile-hung. Tiles are hung over wood and plaster houses to protect them from bad weather. You will see lots of these in Kent.

Weather-boarded. Wooden boards are fixed across the walls to protect them from the weather. You will sometimes see half-weather-boarded houses.

Roofs

Mansard roof. Roof with two slopes on each side, the lower one steeper than the upper.

Hipped roof. Roof with slopes on all sides.

Gabled roof. Roof which slopes on two opposite sides only.

"M"-shaped gable. Two gabled roofs side-by-side.

Crow-steps or corbie-steps. Step shapes at the end of gabled roof.

Dutch gable. Curly shape at the edge of a roof.

Thatch

You can see **thatched roofs** in most parts of Britain. They are usually made from straw, reeds or heather.

Look out for **bird and animal shapes** on the top of thatched buildings. They are often thatchers' trademarks.

Sometimes **church roofs** are thatched, though this is quite rare.

Notice board

Wall

Bus stop

Farm buildings

Here are some things to spot on farms. Some of them are old and quite rare.

Dutch barn. Open-sided barn used for storing hay and straw.

Old granary. Built on mushroom shaped "staddle" stones to keep out damp and rats.

Tithe barn. For storing grain paid to the church in taxes. A tithe was a tenth of each farmer's production.

Wattle and daub. Some old buildings were made by daubing clay or mud over a framework of twigs called wattles.

Silo. Airtight building in which green crops are pressed to make winter food for animals.

Oast house. Used for drying hops, which help to flavour beer. Many are now used as homes.

Cowshed or stable. The half-doors stop the animals getting out but let in fresh air.

Pigsty. Place for keeping pigs. The shed has a small forecourt for feeding.

Henhouse. Sometimes on wheels so it can be moved around. The hens are shut in at night.

Beehive. Usually a white wooden box with compartments inside. The bees' entrance is just above the floor.

Windmills and watermills

Windmills and watermills have been used to grind corn for hundreds of years. People think windmills were introduced into Britain in the 12th century by the Crusaders, who saw them in the Holy Land.

Watermills were built here even earlier, probably by the Romans. Both types of mill were in use until fairly recent times and you will see them in various parts of the country.

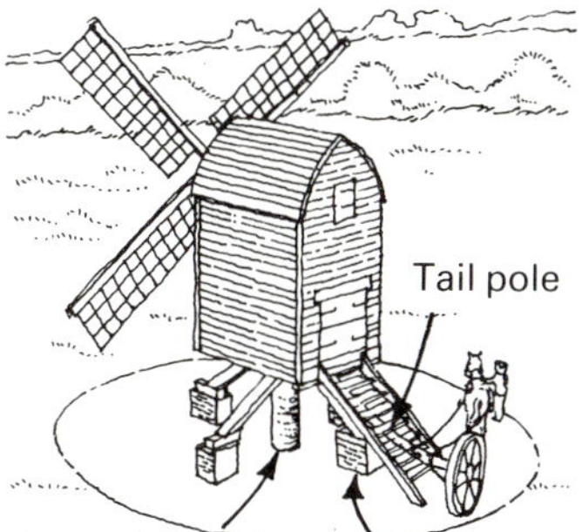

The oldest sort of windmill is the **post mill,** built around a huge wooden post, often a tree trunk. The whole mill revolved around the post so that the sails caught the wind. The miller had to turn the mill himself, or with the help of his horse, by pulling on a "tail pole".

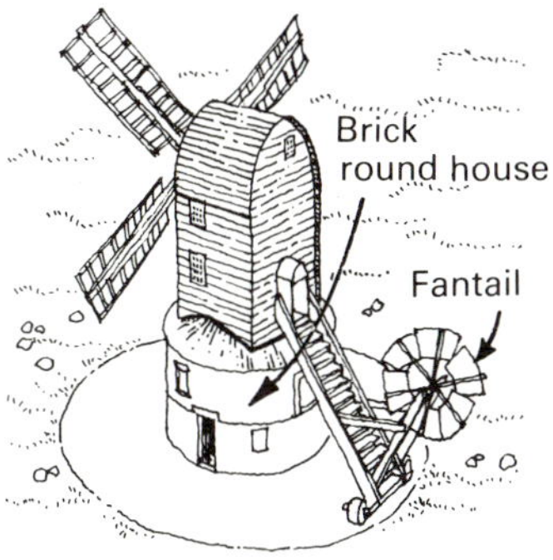

Later post mills often had brick round houses built round their bases for protection, and had "fantails" added. These are small wind vanes which pushed the mill round to the wind automatically.

Smock mills got their name because they are shaped a bit like the smocks country people used to wear. They usually have eight sides and are made of wooden weatherboarding which is painted white or covered in black tar.

The sails were attached to the "cap" and only this part of the mill revolved. Sails were originally covered in canvas and so the miller could still reach them to do repairs tall mills had a gallery round them.

Tower mills also have caps. They are usually bigger than post or smock mills, and are round and built in brick.

More modern sails had hinged shutters a bit like Venetian blinds. Old-fashioned sails sometimes used to get torn off in high winds, but now the shutters could be opened and the wind passed harmlessly through the holes.

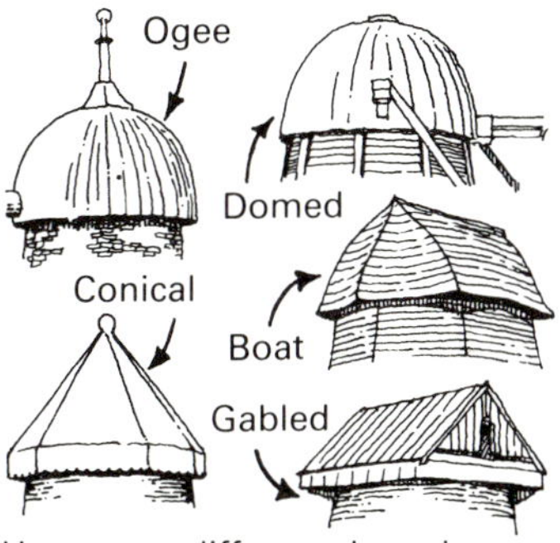

How many different shaped caps can you spot?

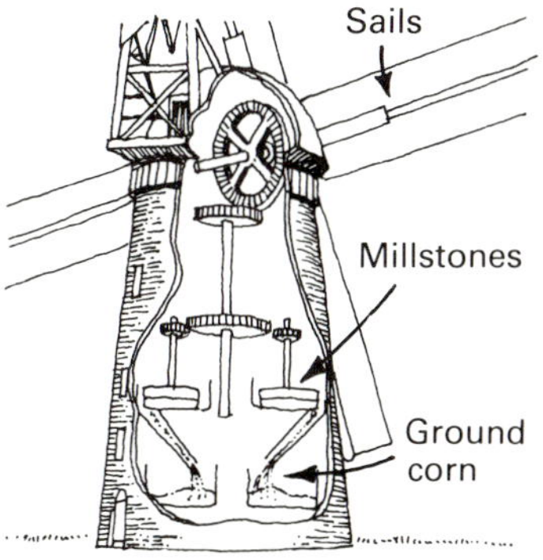

If you go inside a mill, you may be able to see how it worked. The sails were attached to a series of wheels, and the movement of the sails made the wheels turn too. The corn was ground between two millstones.

First, the grain was hoisted up to the top floor, then it was fed slowly down through the millstones and into a bin back on the ground floor.

Windmills were also used to drain water from low-lying, marshy areas, and watermills were used for many things besides grinding corn. They supplied the power for turning early textile and metal working machinery and were even used in making gunpowder and snuff.

Watermills work in the same way as windmills, except that instead of the wind turning sails, flowing water turns a wheel.

Bridges

Clapper bridge. Very old type of bridge made of huge granite slabs resting on rock piles.

Hump-backed bridge. Steeply-arched stone bridge.

Bridge with "V"-shaped alcoves where people can stand to avoid traffic.

Iron bridge. The first ones were built in the early 1800s.

Suspension bridge. A roadway hung on huge cables from turrets at either end.

Cow bridge. Bridge for animals to cross, in places where a main road divides a farmer's land.

Viaduct. Arches which carry a road or railway line across a valley. This is Ribble Head Viaduct in Yorkshire.

Aqueduct. Man-made channel built to carry water. This is the Pont-Cysyllte Aqueduct in Wales. It is 305m long and has 19 arches.

Walls

Laid hedge. The young shoots in a hedge are woven round stakes to make it grow thick.

Dry stone wall. Has no cement between the stones. Needs great skill to build. Common in hilly areas.

Stiles. Steps over walls, fences or hedges. Here are four different kinds.

Crinkle crankle wall. Wiggles in and out. Found mainly in Suffolk, often round orchards.

Kissing gate. Old name for a gate swinging in a forked piece of fence. Animals cannot get through.

Cattle grid. Stops sheep and cows crossing but drivers do not have to open and close gates.

The **overshot mill** has water flowing along a channel above the wheel and falling on to its paddles or troughs.

The wheel of an **undershot mill** is turned by the force of water hitting its paddles from underneath.

London 1

Great Britain's capital city, London, is the 12th largest city in the world and has about seven million people. The oldest part, now the business and banking centre, is called the City. You can still see the remains of a wall the Romans built round it. London's famous shops, theatres and hotels are next to the City, in the West End. Here are some suggestions of things to do and see in London.

Buckingham Palace. The London home of the Queen. If the flag is flying on top it means she is at home. You can visit the Royal Mews where her horses and carriages are kept.

Trafalgar Square. Famous for its pigeons. On the column in the centre is a statue of Admiral Nelson, who defeated the French at the Battle of Trafalgar in 1805.

Piccadilly Circus is the meeting point of six main streets. In the middle is a famous statue of Eros (the Greek god of love) holding a bow and arrow.

The Houses of Parliament consist of the House of Commons and the House of Lords. Members meet here to discuss and pass laws. Big Ben is the bell inside the clock tower.

Westminster Abbey. Since 1066, all English kings and queens have been crowned here. You can see the tombs of most of them and of many other famous people buried here.

The Tower of London. Built as a fortress it later became a prison and place of execution. The Crown Jewels and a collection of arms and armour are now on show here.

St Paul's Cathedral was built to replace old St Paul's, which was burnt down in the Great Fire in 1666. If you go there, visit the Whispering Gallery.

A tour of Westminster Abbey

As you walk round the Abbey see if you can find the tombs and memorials of these people.

In the nave:
Robert Baden-Powell
Winston Churchill
David Livingstone
Charles Darwin.
In the north transept:
William Pitt
Robert Peel
William Gladstone.
In Poets' Corner:
Geoffrey Chaucer
Robert Browning
John Masefield
George Frederick Handel.

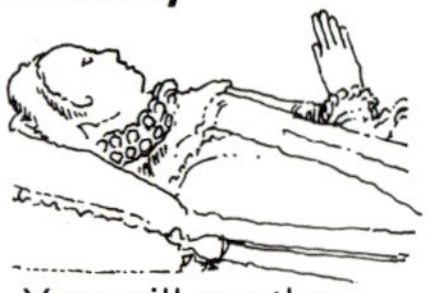

You will see the tomb of Mary Queen of Scots and other kings and queens in the Royal Chapels.

Mary Tudor is buried in the same tomb as her sister, Elizabeth I. See if you can find Mary's name on the tomb.

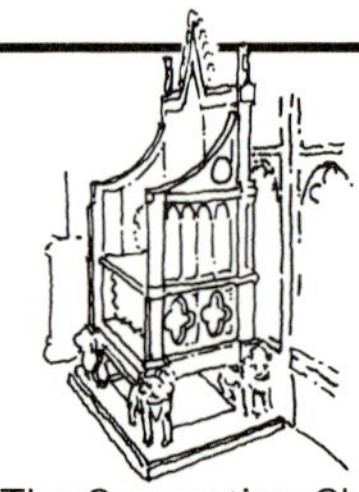

The Coronation Chair has been used at the crowning of English monarchs since 1300.

The Abbey Museum has wax effigies of famous people, which were carried at their funerals.

A tour of the Tower of London

Here are some things to look out for at the Tower.

The Water Gate was known as Traitors' Gate, because prisoners were taken into the Tower there.

There are torture instruments in the Byward Tower. This cramp is called the Scavenger's Daughter.

The axe and block, kept in the Bloody Tower, were used for beheading prisoners on the scaffold site on Tower Green.

The boy princes, Edward V and his brother, Richard, were probably murdered in the Bloody Tower.

The Crown Jewels belong to the state and are used by the royal family only on state occasions.

Eight ravens are kept at the Tower. There is a legend that the Tower will fall if they leave, so their wings are clipped.

Ceremonies and uniforms

The Changing of the Guard at Buckingham Palace. The new guard, led by a band, arrives to take over from the old guard. The ceremony lasts half an hour.

The Changing of the Horse Guards at Horse Guards arch, Whitehall. This gateway is guarded because it was once an entrance to the grounds of the old palace of Whitehall.

Yeomen Warders (Beefeaters) guard the Tower of London. They sometimes wear blue uniforms.

Chelsea Pensioners– summer uniform. These old soldiers live in the Royal Hospital, Chelsea.

The King's Troop, Royal Horse Artillery. Can be seen firing salutes on state occasions in Hyde Park.

Getting around

This sign marks the entrance to the Underground (tube) stations. A quick and easy way to travel.

You can see more if you travel on the top deck of one of London's famous double-deckers.

If you want to take a tour, you can go in a special sightseeing bus with an open top.

A taxi is available for hire when its sign is lit up. Wave your arm to stop one.

Information services

Here are some telephone numbers you can ring for information about London.
222 1234 London Transport Travel Enquiries (information about tubes and buses)
246 8007 Children's London (events of special interest to children)
246 8041 Teletourist (main events of the day)
730 0791 London Tourist Board Information Bureau
If you are telephoning from outside London dial **01** before these numbers.

London's history

1

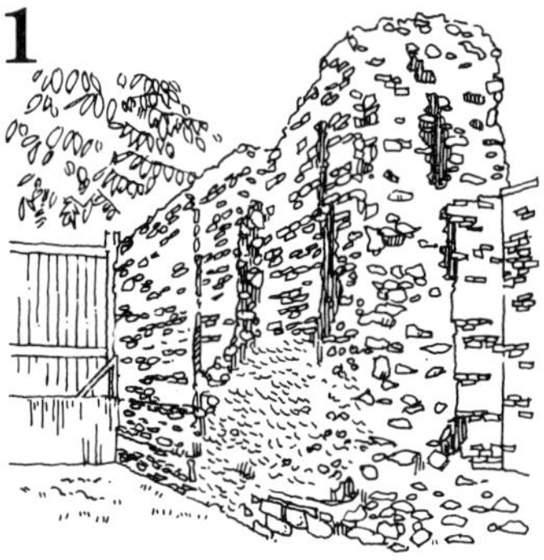

The Romans founded *Londinium* in AD 43. The wall they built contained the town for 1,000 years. At the Museum of London you can see part of the wall with an explanation of how it was built.

2

In AD 61 Queen Boudicca led an unsuccessful revolt of native tribes against the Romans. You can see a statue of her on Westminster Bridge.

3

By the time of the Tudors, London had grown beyond the old Roman walls, to the west. Staple Inn, in Holborn, was built in 1586 and gives an idea of what London used to look like. Look out for other black and white timbered buildings. They are all in or near the City.

4

In 1666 the Great Fire of London started in a baker's shop in Pudding Lane and most of London burnt down. There is a reconstruction of the fire at the Museum of London. Afterwards, all buildings had to be built in brick or stone.

5

After the fire, Sir Christopher Wren was given the job of rebuilding St Paul's and the City churches. See how many different types of steeple you can spot. Today the churches are often used for concerts.

6

In the 18th century many houses were built in long terraces or around squares with a private garden in the middle. Originally these were the homes of dukes and earls, though some are now offices.

7

Many houses had wide doorways so that sedan chairs could be carried into the hall.

8

Today you will see many tall new buildings. The Barbican, in the City, was built on the site where the first bomb fell in World War II. It has flats, shops, a theatre and the Museum of London.

Famous houses

▲ **10 Downing Street** is where the Prime Minister lives. It is just off Whitehall.

▲ **Lambeth Palace** has been the London home of the Archbishop of Canterbury for 750 years.

▶ The Lord Mayor of London lives in the **Mansion House** during his one-year term of office. If you are in London on the second Saturday in November, you can watch the celebrations of the Lord Mayor's Show.

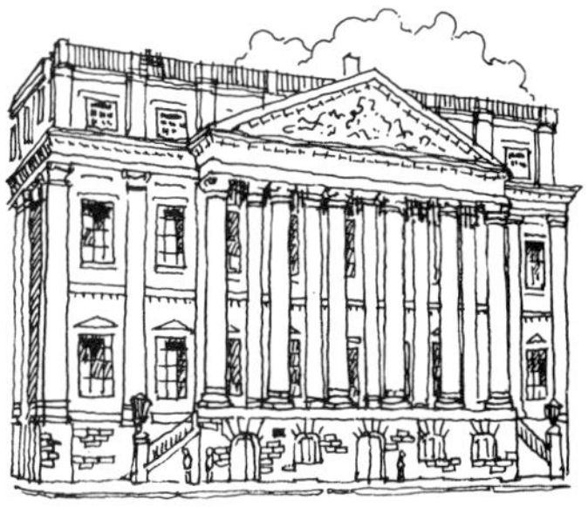

◀ **Kensington Palace** was the main private home of the monarch from 1689 to 1760, when Buckingham Palace was bought. Queen Victoria was born here and you can visit the state apartments.

London's horses

Wealthy people used to keep their horses in mews – stables at the back of grand houses. Many mews have been converted into houses.

People ride for pleasure in Rotten Row in Hyde Park. The name comes from *Route du Roi* which is French for the King's Road.

London's police stations have stables for 200 horses. Police horses are named according to the year they join the force, e.g. all 1980 names begin with I.

Young and Co. is one of the breweries that still delivers beer by shire-horse and dray. The horses are black with white socks.

In the Royal Mews you can see the Queen's horses and gold state coach used for coronations. It takes eight horses to pull it.

Troopers of the Household Cavalry exercise in Hyde Park every morning before riding to Whitehall for the Changing of the Horse Guards.

London 2

The River Thames

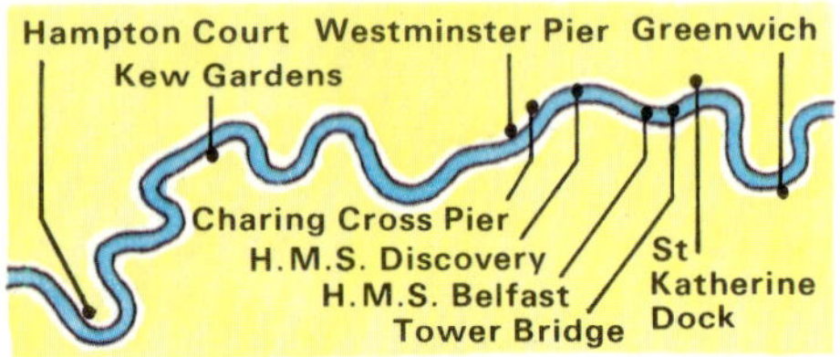

London grew up along the Thames and you can see some interesting places on its banks. This map marks the places mentioned below.

In the summer, you can take **boat tours** starting from Charing Cross or Westminster Piers.

H.M.S. Discovery was the ship used on Scott's Antarctic expedition (1901–4). It is now a museum.

H.M.S. Belfast, the largest cruiser ever built for the Royal Navy, is now used as a Royal Navy Museum.

The Cutty Sark, on show at Greenwich Pier, is an old "clipper" ship which was used for carrying tea.

Tower Bridge was built in 1894. It opens to let big ships through, though very few come this far up the river now.

St Katherine Dock used to be a place where ships unloaded, but is now a yachting marina with a hotel, pubs and shops. There are lots of boats to see, including old Thames sailing barges and a lightship.

The Old Royal Observatory in Greenwich Park is where Greenwich Mean Time is measured from.

Kew Gardens have a vast collection of trees and plants. The glass palm house above, has exotic tropical plants.

Hampton Court Palace, built in 1515, is full of treasures and has lovely gardens, which include a maze.

Viewpoints

A good way of getting to know a city is to go to a high point from which you can get a good view.

Primrose Hill. From here and from nearby Hampstead Heath, you can look south over London for a long way. Good places for flying kites.

Westminster Cathedral. Main Roman Catholic Church. Go to top of tower by lift for view of central London.

The Monument. Commemorates Fire of London in 1666. Climb up steps inside hollow column for view of City.

St Paul's Cathedral. Walk round the outside of the dome or go right up to the ball 112m above the ground.

Post Office Tower. Can be seen from most other high points. Now closed.

Parks

London is full of parks, gardens and green open spaces. Among them are ten big royal parks which were once the grounds of royal palaces. Many of them have boating ponds, lakes, playgrounds, statues and interesting birds and animals.

In **St James's** one of the royal parks, you can see pelicans and unusual ducks and geese which nest on an island in the lake.

This statue of Peter Pan stands near the Long Water in **Kensington Gardens** which join on to Hyde Park.

In **Richmond Park,** herds of fallow and red deer roam wild. If you are lucky you might also see a fox or weasel.

Regent's Park contains London Zoo. It is one of the biggest zoos in the world and has a collection of over 6,600 animals.

In **Crystal Palace Park,** there are life-size models of dinosaurs on islands in the boating lake.

Interesting museums

There are so many museums in London that it would take years to see them all. The British Museum and the Victoria and Albert are two of the most famous. Here are some things from other museums you might find interesting.

Museum of London. Illustrates the history of London. This is the Lord Mayor of London's state coach.

Imperial War Museum. Weapons, models, uniforms, photographs from all wars involving Britain, since 1914.

Natural History Museum. Dinosaur skeletons, fossils and stuffed animals, birds and reptiles.

Science Museum. Models and machines showing the history of science. This is a model of the Apollo 10 space capsule.

Geological Museum. Gold, diamonds, precious stones, rocks and fossils and "Story of the Earth" exhibition.

Horniman Museum. Arts and crafts and natural history. These are from the musical instruments section.

Bethnal Green Museum. A museum of childhood showing old-fashioned toys, dolls and doll's houses.

Pollock's Toy Museum specialises in model theatres, dolls, teddy bears and other toys. It also has a shop.

Planetarium. An expert gives a commentary while images of the night sky are projected onto the domed ceiling.

Madame Tussauds. Life-size wax figures of famous people, including a Chamber of Horrors.

London Dungeon. Very gruesome displays showing gory scenes from British history.

Famous streets, shops and markets

Whitehall is where the main government offices are. The monument in the centre is called the Cenotaph.

Fleet Street is where many newspapers have their head offices. Look for their names on the buildings.

Oxford Street has many big department stores and is probably the busiest shopping street in London.

Harrods is one of the most famous shops in the world. They claim they will get anything you want to buy.

Fortnum and Mason has an exotic food hall, selling food from all over the world. It has a special clock outside.

Hamleys in Regent Street is a famous toy shop which sells every kind of toy and game you can imagine.

Portobello Road Market. On Saturdays the road is full of stalls selling antiques and all kinds of junk.

Petticoat Lane Market is open only on Sunday mornings. It sells mainly household goods.

Smithfield Market is the biggest meat market in the world. It is at its busiest in the very early morning.

Fun things to do in London

Music

Robert Mayer Children's Concerts, Royal Festival Hall, South Bank, SE1. Tel: 928 3191. Waterloo tube. Classical music concerts for 8-12 year olds – six Saturday mornings between October and March. Write for tickets to BBC, Yalding House, 156 Gt Portland St, W1.

Films

Odeon Cinema, St Martin's Lane, WC2. Tel: 836 0691. Leicester Sq. tube. Disney films. *Mickey Mouse Club* (join by showing four ticket stubs) puts you on mailing list. *Birthday Club* (join by writing name and date of birth in special book) gets you a free ticket to a Saturday show for your birthday.

ICA Cinema, Nash House, The Mall, SW1. Tel: 930 3647. Charing Cross tube. Children's films at weekends: a month of science fiction, a month of cartoons, etc. Films introduced by people involved in making them. *Children's Cinema Club* (free membership when you buy a ticket) puts you on mailing list and allows you to take in one adult non-member.

Junior NFT, National Film Theatre, South Bank, SE1. Waterloo tube. Wide selection of films for under-16s at weekends (members only). Tel: 437 4355 for details.

London Experience, 7 Coventry St, W1. Tel: 437 1533. Piccadilly Circus tube. Story of London in films and slides. Special effects. Daily shows.

Theatres

Little Angel Marionette Theatre, Dagmar Passage, off Cross St, N1. Tel: 226 1787. Highbury tube. Weekend puppet theatre with separate shows for under-5s and over-5s. Performances every day at holiday times.

Unicorn Theatre, 6 Gt Newport St, WC2. Tel: 836 3334. Leicester Sq. tube. Plays for 4-12 year olds. Also runs *Unicorn Theatre Club* for workshops in acrobatics, stage fighting, make-up, etc; puppet shows, conjurors, competitions.

Riverside Studios, Crisp Rd, W6. Tel: 748 3354. Hammersmith tube. Plays for children at weekends, workshops in dance and music, films, etc.

Inter-Action Trust Ltd, 15 Wilkin St, NW5. Tel: 485 0881. Kentish Town tube. Community arts centre with workshops in printing and silk-screening, and a City Farm. Also a Fun Art bus from which plays are performed in the streets.

Zoos

XYZ Club, London Zoo, Regent's Park, NW1. Tel: 722 3333. Camden Town tube. Membership gives you six free tickets to the zoo a year and magazines with news of competitions and special events such as trips to other zoos. Bureau gives information and advice on animals and pets.

Crystal Palace Park and **Battersea Park** have smaller zoos, open in summer.

If you are telephoning from outside London dial **01** before these numbers.

Street furniture

There are many odd objects in London's streets that are quite difficult to spot. Try looking for some of these.

Before free state schools, poor children went to **charity schools.** These had carvings of children on their buildings.

Blue plaques are put on houses to show where famous people lived. Charles Dickens lived at 48 Doughty Street.

Lions appear in many places in London. You can see sculptures of lions in Trafalgar Square and on Westminster Bridge, and lions' heads on the Embankment.

Shops with the **purveyors' sign** above the door supply goods to the royal family.

London has many **unusual clocks.** On Liberty's store, in Regent Street, St George chases the dragon on the stroke of every hour.

Many **bollards** are made from old ships' cannons. There is often a cannon ball on top.

You can see **animals on old iron lamp-posts** like these by the Thames.

Griffins mark the boundaries of the City of London.

In Piccadilly, near Hyde Park Corner, is the **porters' rest**: a shoulder-high wooden slab where porters could rest their load.

Metal plaques in the ground mark the route of the Queen's Silver Jubilee Walkway, made in 1977 to celebrate her 25-year reign.

The **Whittington Stone,** Highgate Hill, marks the spot where Dick Whittington heard Bow Bells call "Turn again, Whittington".

London Transport Museum

The transport museum, in Covent Garden, shows you the history of transport in London over the past 150 years.

▲ You can see a replica of the first horse-drawn omnibus. Built by George Shillibeer, it made its first run in 1829.

▲ The first standard motor bus, the 'B' type, was introduced in 1910. Many were used overseas to carry troops in World War I.

◀ This Metropolitan Railway steam locomotive, built in 1866, was used on the Circle line of the Underground until the line was electrified in 1905.

Fun Things To Do

British Rail stopped using **steam trains** in 1968. But they have now become so popular that railway enthusiasts are allowed to run special excursions on main lines. There are also several private lines. This train is in Oakworth station on the private Keighley and Worth Valley line.

In Wales, there are several **small steam railways.** They run on narrow-gauge tracks and operate mainly in the summer.

There are several **miniature railways** in Britain, but the Romney, Hythe and Dymchurch line in Kent is the world's only mainline miniature railway.

A **camera obscura** is a room used as a camera. Images from outside the room are reflected on to a table.

Cheddar, in Somerset, is one of the places where you can see **caves** with stalagmites and stalactites.

In petrifying **wells** objects are coated in stone by lime in the water. You can see one at Knaresborough (Yorks).

The **Dr Who Exhibition** in Blackpool has models and monsters used in the filming of the B.B.C. television series.

You can meet Santa Claus and ride on his sleigh at any time of the year in **Santa Claus Land,** at Aviemore in Scotland.

This Viking ship is at **Thorpe Park,** near Staines, which shows the history of Britain as a seafaring nation.

There are several **old ships** you can go aboard. This is H.M.S. Victory, Nelson's flagship at the Battle of Trafalgar, at Portsmouth.

You can go for **boat trips** on most big lakes and rivers. Look out for the monster if you go on Loch Ness.

In **model villages,** everything is on a miniature scale so that you feel like a giant. At Bekonscot in Buckinghamshire the village includes a castle, a zoo and a railway.

At most **airports** there is a viewing platform from which you can watch aeroplanes taking off and landing.

Watching people at work

Many factories and craft centres will let you come and watch people at work, but you often have to make a special appointment, well in advance. Local tourist boards can usually give you a list of such places. Here are some activities that you can usually go and watch without making arrangements in advance.

Several well-known **glass factories,** such as Dartington (Devon) and Caithness (Scotland), give tours which show you every stage in the process of making glass.

You can often visit **potteries** and watch people making pots. Look out for signs as you travel around.

In villages, you can sometimes see **blacksmiths** at work, making horseshoes and iron objects.

Many **windmills** have recently been restored. Here at North Leverton in Nottinghamshire, the mill grinds corn.

Zoos and safari parks

By far the largest collection of birds and animals is the British national collection at London Zoo, but there are a large number of smaller collections throughout the rest of Britain. Here are a few suggestions of interesting places to visit.

The Lions of Longleat (opened 1966) was the first drive-through safari park in Europe. At first it had only lions but now it has a wide variety of birds and animals, mainly from Africa.

Most zoos have an aquarium, but one of the best is at Chester (the second largest zoo in the country), where you can see sea-horses.

Feeding times for the different animals are usually shown on notice boards. In Edinburgh, the penguins parade through the zoo before they are fed.

Bristol Zoo, the second oldest in Britain, is one of the few in the world which has white tigers.

Whipsnade zoo specializes in herds of animals. It has several rare species, including white rhinos.

Twycross zoo park has the best collection of apes and monkeys in Britain. These are rare proboscis monkeys.

Several zoos and safari parks now have dolphinaria where you can see dolphins performing tricks. They jump high out of the water and throw and catch balls.

Most zoos have a pets' corner or childrens zoo. These are special areas where you can get a closer look at the animals, and often you are allowed to stroke them.

Interesting museums

You may think that museums are boring, but there are lots of really exciting ones. Here are a few. Most of these specialize in a particular subject and in several you can touch the exhibits and even have rides on them.

The **National Railway Museum** in York has the largest collection of railway relics in Britain. Several engines are still in working order.

Noah's Arks have been popular toys for about 200 years. This is in Edinburgh's **Museum of Childhood.**

The **Llandudno Doll Museum** has over 1,000 dolls. This is a doll, used by tailors to model fashions.

The **Museum of Costume** in Bath shows fashionable dress from the 17th century onwards.

The **National Motor Museum** at Beaulieu tells the story of motoring from 1895 to modern times. Over 200 vehicles are on display.

There was once a famous ship-building yard at **Buckler's Hard.** Now its Maritime Museum displays models of the ships once built here.

The **Ironbridge Gorge Museum** is an open-air museum which covers the area around the world's first iron bridge. It tells you about industry in the past.

At the **Gladstone Pottery Museum** in Staffordshire, you can see demonstrations of traditional pottery making. The pots used to be fired in these "bottle ovens".

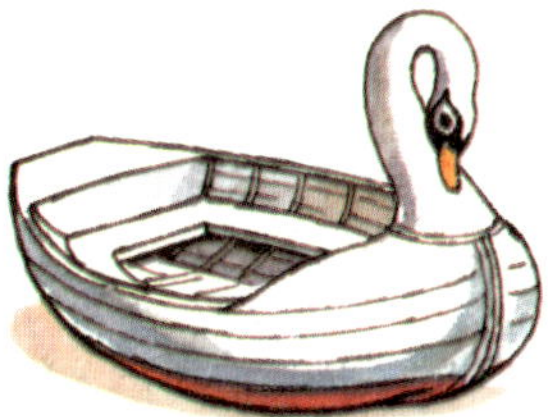

This is one of the many unusual boats on show at **Exeter Maritime Museum.** The larger boats are afloat and you can go aboard and explore them.

At the **Tramway Museum,** Crich, Derbyshire you can take rides on horse-drawn, steam and electric trams, all of which were once used in big cities.

This old market hall is in the **Weald and Downland Open-Air Museum** in Sussex. The museum rescues and rebuilds historic buildings from south-east England.

At the **Beamish North of England Open-Air Museum** you can see cottages and farms as they were 100 years ago. There is also a steam train, an old station and a colliery.

The historic aeroplanes in the **Shuttleworth Collection,** near Biggleswade, are kept in working order.

The **Waterways Museum** at Stoke Bruerne tells you about life on the canals. This is the inside of a narrow boat.

The **Yorkshire Fire Museum** at Batley has the largest collection of old fire engines on public view in Britain.

The **Musical Museum** at Brentford in Middlesex has a fascinating collection of automatic pianos, organs and music boxes. All of them are in working order.

The **American Museum** in Bath shows how people in America have lived over the past few hundred years. This is a full-size model of a Red Indian tepee.

Wildlife parks

The Norfolk Wildlife Park and Pheasant Trust has the largest collection of European animals, like this badger, in the world. It also has many rare species of pheasants.

In the Highland Wildlife Park you can see a wide selection of animals that either used to live in the area or, like this wild cat, still do but are not easy to see.

The Slimbridge Wildfowl Refuge has the world's largest display of flamingoes, geese, swans and ducks. This is the brilliantly coloured mandarin duck.

Nature trails

Many parks and forests have nature trails which you can follow. Signs and leaflets tell you about the birds, animals and plants you might see.

Farm parks

If you are interested in farms and farm animals, you might enjoy a visit to a farm park. At Easton Farm Park, Suffolk, you can watch the herd of cows being milked.

Many farm parks and farm museums show you old-fashioned methods of farming. Many things that used to be done by hand are now done by machine.

Special collections

The Otter Trust in Suffolk protects and breeds otters, which are endangered animals.

Worldwide Butterflies in Dorset has the biggest collection of living butterflies in Britain.

The Falconry Centre, Gloucestershire has flying falcon displays and a superb collection of birds of prey.

Festivals, Shows and Sporting Events

Shows and festivals are often advertised on posters and in newspapers. Tourist offices and libraries can usually tell you about special events happening in their areas. For some of the big events it is best to buy tickets in advance.

The **Edinburgh Festival** is one of the biggest arts festivals in the world. It takes place every year in August and September. There are plays, films, concerts and exhibitions, and a military tattoo performed at the castle.

At the **Farnborough Air Show**, held in July, you can see all kinds of aircraft. The Red Arrow R.A.F. squadron, which specializes in aerobatics, gives flying displays.

The **Royal Tournament** is a display of military skills, including competitions between groups of soldiers, held at Earls Court in London in July.

The Queen's official birthday is celebrated every year at the **Trooping of the Colour**. This is on the second Saturday in June at Horse Guards Parade, London.

The **Royal National Eisteddfod** of Wales is a festival of Welsh music and poetry. It is held in August and takes place in a different Welsh town each year.

Car manufacturers from all over the world show off their latest cars every October at the **International Motor Show** at the Exhibition Centre, Birmingham.

County **agricultural shows** are held throughout Britain in the summer months. Farmers compete to win prizes for the best animals.

Dancing round a maypole on 1 May is an ancient custom. Look out for it in country villages.

Morris dancers often appear at local festivals. They wear special costumes with bells on their legs.

Travelling **fairs** visit most towns during the year. Some places, like Oxford, have a medieval fair in summer.

Sheep dog trials test how good dogs are at rounding up sheep. National trials are held every summer.

Dogs of all kinds can be seen at **Cruft's International Dog Show** held every February at Olympia, London.

The **Chelsea Flower Show** is world famous. It is held in the gardens of Chelsea Royal Hospital in London every May.

Circuses began in Britain in the 1770s. There are now 23 circus groups which travel round the country giving shows.

On 5 November, people light **bonfires and fireworks** in memory of Guy Fawkes' attempt to blow up the Houses of Parliament in 1605.

On Christmas Eve, **carol singers** traditionally go round and sing outside people's houses.

In Scotland, there are **Highland Gatherings** where you can see piping and dancing and athletic contests.

Rowing teams from all over the world compete in the famous **regatta** held on the Thames at Henley.

Veteran cars can be seen taking part in the R.A.C. London to Brighton Run in November.

Sports

The soccer (football) season lasts from August to April. The highlight of the season is the F.A. Cup Final held at Wembley Stadium in London in May.

Amateur, 15-a-side teams play Rugby Union and, in the north of England, professional 13-a-side teams play Rugby League. You can see both every winter Saturday.

Horse races are held all year round. The famous races are the Derby, first held in 1780, and now run every year in June, and the Grand National, which is run in April.

Britain's round of the world motor-racing drivers' championships is the John Player Grand Prix. It is usually held in July at either Brands Hatch or Silverstone motor racing tracks.

In the summer, county cricket teams play in various competitions, like the Benson and Hedges Cup and the Nat. West. Cup. There are also test matches against other countries.

The world's top tennis players come to Wimbledon every year for the Lawn Tennis Championships. They are held in the last week of June and the first week of July.

World championship motor cycle races are held at major race tracks. Speedway racing takes place most weeks. Check local papers for dates and places.

The main showjumping events are the Royal International Horse Show in July and the Horse of the Year Show in October. Both are at Wembley, London.

The Seaside

1

Sea bathing was almost unheard of in Britain until the early 1700s. Then, doctors decided that going in the sea and even drinking sea water were good for the health and wealthy people started going to the coast. This picture shows Scarborough, one of the first seaside resorts, in the 1770s. The carts are bathing machines which were dragged out to sea by horses and used by people to bathe from.

2

In the early 1800s doctors discovered that sea air was healthy too. Elegant houses were built facing the sea and promenades were built along the sea front. Places like Brighton and Weymouth became fashionable when royalty went there. After the railways were built in the mid 1800s many resorts grew in popularity as more and more people were able to get to the coast.

3

As early as 1800, people were amusing themselves on the beach by taking donkey rides, which were probably introduced by gypsies. Later, some beaches had carriages pulled by goats for children to ride in. Punch and Judy shows were also popular.

4

Piers were originally built as landing stages for boats, but they gradually became places where people went to enjoy themselves. Many were built in the 1880s and most had a pavilion on them with things like aquaria, flea circuses and souvenir shops inside.

5

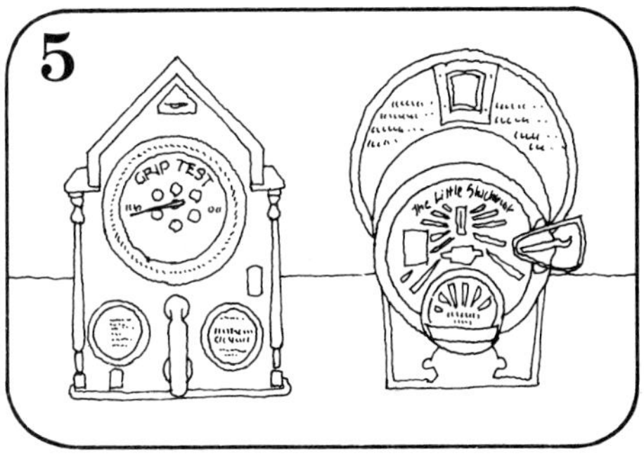

There were penny slot machines on piers from about 1900 on. A popular one was the electric shock machine, which people thought cured various illnesses. On Brighton Palace Pier there is a slot machine museum. You can borrow old pennies to work the machines.

Looking at rocks

The seaside is a particularly good place for looking at rocks. You can often see different patterns and colours in the cliffs and find fossils or unusual pebbles on the beach.

Fossils are the remains of plants and animals which were squashed amongst the rocks when they were being made. Here are two fairly common kinds.

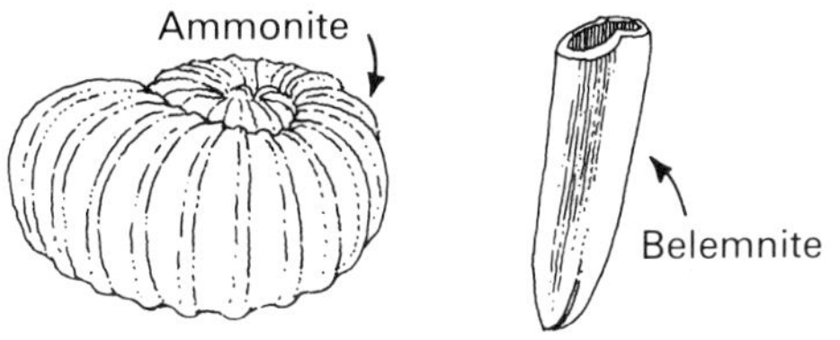

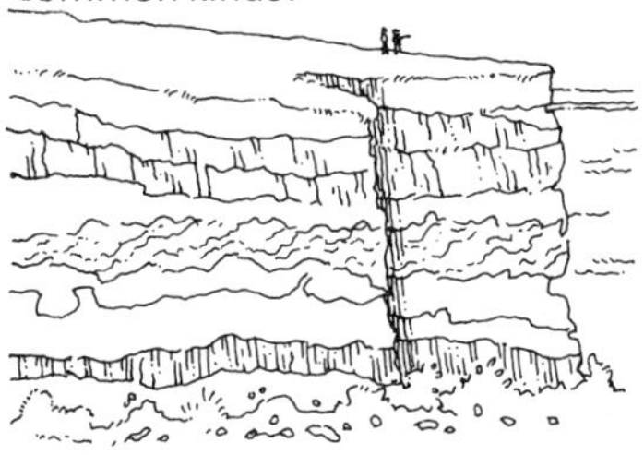

You can often see **layers** in the cliffs. These show they are sedimentary rocks, which were made under the sea.

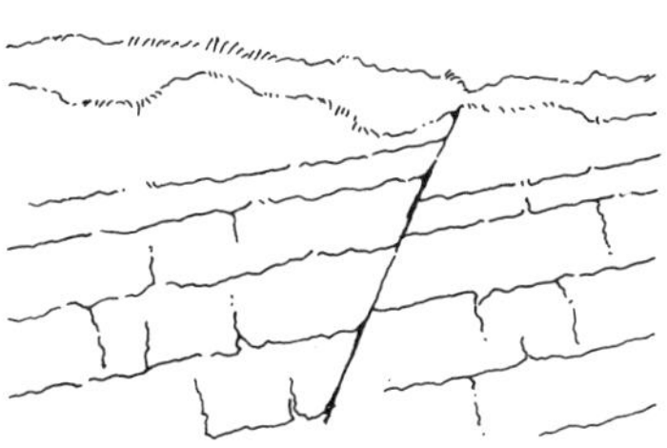

Look out for places where earth movements have made the rocks split and shift, causing a break or **fault** in the layers.

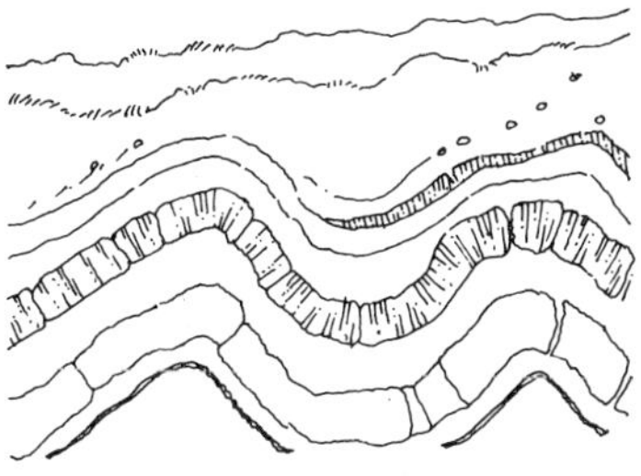

Movements inside the earth also make **folds** in the rocks. Upward folds are called anticlines and downward folds synclines.

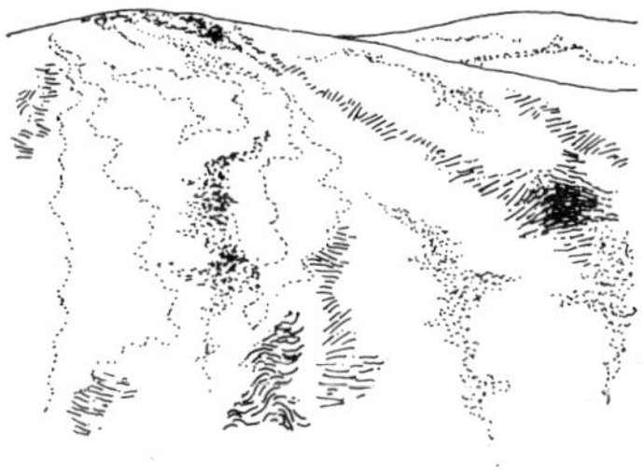

In some places the sand is unusual colours. Alum Bay, on the Isle of Wight, has 12 **different coloured sands.**

Guarding the coast

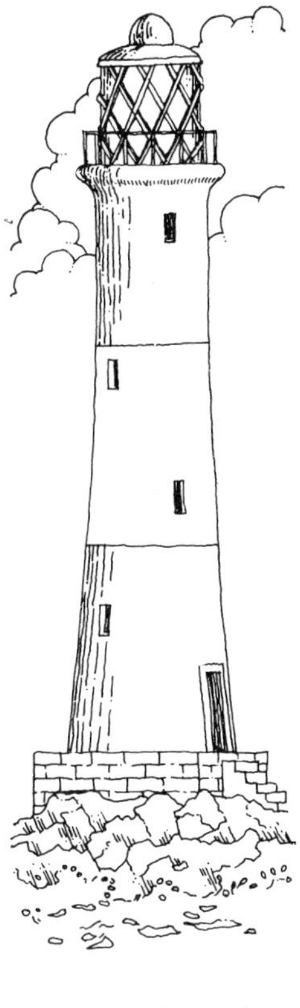

You can look round about 80 of Britain's **lighthouses.** For a list write to the Public Relations Officer, Trinity House, Tower Hill, London EC3N 4DH.

Britain has about 200 **lifeboat stations**. You can go inside most of them and see the boat and other equipment, which are always kept ready for an emergency.

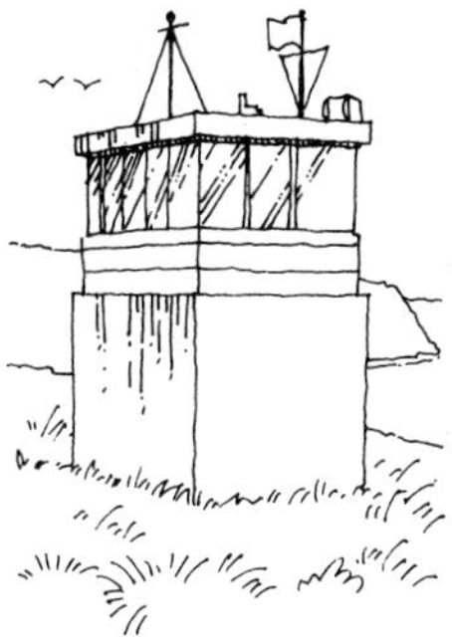

Look out for radio masts on **coastguard stations.** If a ship is in distress, it can send a signal to the coastguards and they will call out the lifeboat.

Martello towers are round forts which were built along the south-east coast in the early 1800s, when people thought Napoleon might try to invade Britain.

You may see squat concrete buildings like this around the coast too. They are called **pill-boxes,** and were built as look-out posts during World War II.

In the Countryside

Although Britain has a large population for its size, there are still many unspoilt areas of countryside that you can explore.

Some of the best places to go are those which are looked after by organizations like the ones mentioned on this page. The addresses of the organizations are on page 79 and you can write to them for further information. National and regional tourist offices (addresses on page 79) will also give you details.

Remember, you always stand a much better chance of getting a quick reply to your letter if you enclose a large, stamped, self-addressed envelope.

National parks

There are ten national parks in England and Wales. They are all named on the maps in this book, and coloured in green. They are not like ordinary parks, but are large areas of open countryside, usually moorland, mountain, woodland or sea, but with whole towns and villages too.

Booklets describing the parks tell you about the interesting things to see and do, whether there are facilities for things like camping, pony trekking or fishing, and give you information on the parks' animal and plant life, geology and history.

For general information you can write to the Countryside Commission, or for details and booklets about a specific park write to the main information centre in that park.

You will see the symbols of the different parks on their boundaries, at information centres in the parks and on pamphlets.

Areas of outstanding natural beauty

In addition to the national parks, there are several smaller "areas of outstanding natural beauty" in England and Wales where industrial development is discouraged. These are marked in the same colour as the national parks on the maps in this book.

Forest parks

Scotland, England and Wales have eight forest parks: Glenmore, Argyll, Queen Elizabeth, Galloway, Border, Dean, New Forest and Snowdonia. They are all named on our maps.

The main purpose of the parks is to grow timber, but many areas are open to the public for walking, camping, picnicking and, in some places, things like wayfaring, canoeing, birdwatching, etc. There are many signposted forest walks and nature trails, and you can buy descriptive leaflets from the visitors' centres.

For details of both forest parks and smaller forests write to the Forestry Commission or, in Northern Ireland, to the Department of Agriculture (Northern Ireland).

Country parks

These are areas of countryside usually near large towns. Some are small areas of wood or open parkland where you can walk or picnic, others have facilities for doing sports like sailing or riding and have museums or zoos.

For information on country parks write to the Countryside Commission in England and Wales, the Countryside Commission for Scotland in Scotland and the Department of the Environment in Northern Ireland.

The National Trust

Much of Britain's land is owned by the National Trust, National Trust for Scotland and the National Trust for Northern Ireland. The Trusts preserve places of natural beauty and interesting old houses and buildings.

There is a special membership scheme for people under 23, which gives you free entry to all the Trusts' properties.

Long distance paths

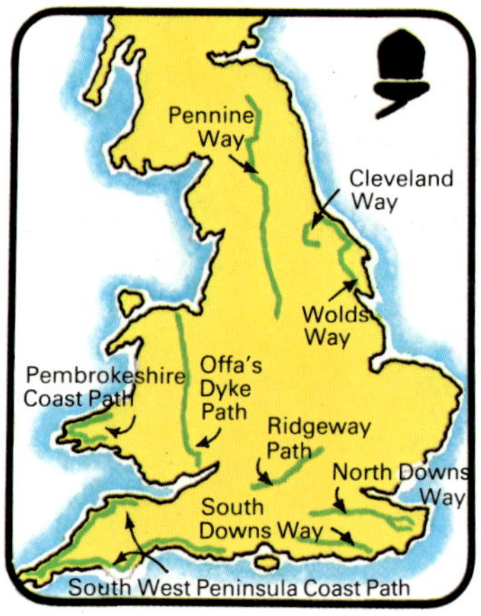

These paths have been planned so that people can walk through long stretches of countryside avoiding major towns and roads. Although it takes days, or even weeks, to walk some of them, it is often possible to go just a short way along them. All the paths are signposted with an acorn symbol. Write to the Countryside Commission for leaflets and guide books.

In Northern Ireland there is a 725km long footpath called the Ulster Way, which goes through all the six counties in the province. For information write to the Sports Council for Northern Ireland (address on page 37).

You can find out about organized walks and walking holidays on page 36.

Nature trails

A nature trail is a signposted walk through an area with interesting animal, bird or plant life, or geology. There are often signboards on the route explaining what you are passing, or you can buy a leaflet describing the trail.

Nature trails are marked on our maps with this paw mark symbol: 🐾 For details of more trails you can write to the Forestry Commission, the Department of Agriculture in Northern Ireland, the Nature Conservancy Councils, the National Trusts and tourist boards.

Here are examples of some of the things you might see on a nature trail. These are taken from a trail in the Gosford Forest Park in Northern Ireland.

A "ha ha": a fence at the bottom of a ditch. It stops cattle from straying but does not spoil the view.

Small holes in the bark of sequoia trees, made by nesting tree creepers.

Moss growing on the north side of an oak tree, which is shaded from the sun.

Poplars: matches and dart boards are often made from these trees.

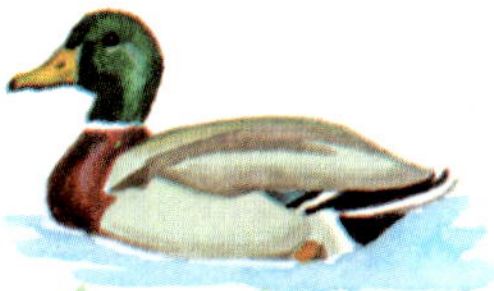

Pond with different species of duck. This is a male mallard.

Traces of a volcanic rock called basalt, where the river has worn away the soil.

A badger sett. Look for tracks nearby and bedding piled at the entrance.

Sometimes kingfishers are seen on this section of the river.

A coast redwood. Coast redwoods are the tallest trees in the world.

A giant sequoia. Giant sequoias are the bulkiest trees in the world.

Irish yews. The leaves and berries are very poisonous.

Many species of bird live among the trees. This is a long-eared owl.

Farm trails

These are rather like nature trails, but take you around farmland so that you can see where the animals live and how the farm works. See Fun Things to Do on page 31 for farm parks. Farms you can visit are marked on our maps by this tractor symbol: 🚜 . For more information you can write to the tourist boards or the Countryside Commissions.

Nature reserves

Many areas have been established as national or local nature reserves. They are protected because they have rare or interesting geology, animal, bird or plant life. The public is allowed to visit many of the reserves, though there are strict rules about where you can walk so as not to disturb or endanger the wildlife.

For lists of nature reserves write to the Nature Conservancy Councils in England, Scotland and Wales and the Department of the Environment in Northern Ireland.

Bird sanctuaries

These are like nature reserves but are specially for birds. Rare species are helped to survive and all birds can nest and breed there. Some of the sanctuaries are marked on our maps with this bird symbol: 🐦 .

Pink-footed goose

Many sanctuaries are round the coast or at reservoirs. Write to the Water Space Amenity Commission for lists of reservoirs where you can watch birds in England and Wales.

The Wildfowl Trust runs seven refuges for birds in England and Scotland. You can watch swans, geese and ducks, some of them very rare, from specially constructed hides.

Helping to conserve nature

If you want to learn more about nature and help preserve beautiful areas of the countryside or protect endangered species of animal or bird from extinction, you can write to one of the clubs and associations listed below. They are all different, but here are some examples of the type of things you can do by becoming a member.

Grey seals – an endangered species

You can go on field trips and expeditions to nature reserves and sanctuaries, learn about nature and conservation from newsletters and magazines, go on field study courses and holidays and, in some cases, help in a very practical way by doing jobs like clearing ponds, planting trees or making footpaths.

Watch Club
Wildlife Youth Service
British Naturalists' Association
National Trust
British Trust for Conservation Volunteers
Field Studies Council
Young Ornithologists' Club
British Trust for Ornithology

FOLLOW THE COUNTRY CODE

Guard against all risk of fire
Fasten all gates
Keep dogs under proper control
Keep to the paths across farm land
Avoid damaging fences, hedges and walls
Leave no litter
Safeguard water supplies
Protect wild life, wild plants and trees
Go carefully on country roads
Respect the life of the countryside

Outdoor Activities and Holidays

There are lots of sports and activites you can do outdoors in Britain, but it is often difficult to do them on your own. Here are the names and addresses of organizations you can write to for information. You will usually find it is best to join a club, where you can get training and sometimes go on courses and full length holidays.

National and regional tourist boards (addresses on page 79) will also tell you what sports you can do in their areas and give details of special interest and activity holidays.

Always remember to enclose a stamped, self-addressed envelope when you write off for information.

Walking

Many tourist boards produce good booklets describing walks in their areas, from easy, signposted trails to proper hill walks. You can get details of long distance paths in England and Wales from the Countryside Commission (address on page 79) and in Northern Ireland from the Sports Council (address on opposite page). For forest walks write to the Forestry Commission (page 79) or, in Northern Ireland, to the Department of Agriculture (Northern Ireland) (page 79).

The Ramblers' Association fights for the right of the public to walk through the countryside and has several local groups. You can become a junior member.

The Youth Hostels Association provides cheap overnight accommodation in dormitories for people who are exploring out-of-the-way country areas. You have to be accompanied by an adult until you are 12.

The Ramblers' Association and Youth Hostels Association both organize walking holidays and if you want to take up hill walking one of these would be a good introduction. Walking can be much more dangerous than it sounds, usually because of treacherous weather conditions, and you should never set out alone.

Addresses:
Ramblers' Association, 1/5 Wandsworth Road, London SW8 2LJ
Youth Hostels Association (England and Wales), Trevelyan House, St Albans, Herts. AL1 2DY
Scottish Youth Hostels Association, 7 Glebe Crescent, Stirling FK8 2JA
Youth Hostel Association of Northern Ireland, 56 Bradbury Place, Belfast BT7 1RU

Wayfaring and Orienteering

In wayfaring, instead of following a signposted path as on a nature trail, you use a map to find your own way round a specially laid out course, usually in a forest. Write to the Forestry Commission for details.

Orienteering is a more advanced form of wayfaring and you can compete against other people in trying to get round the course in the fastest possible time. Write to the British Orienteering Federation, Lea Green, Near Matlock, Derbys. DE4 5GJ.

Camping

Camping gives you the freedom to explore out-of-the-way places and follow your outdoor interests cheaply. The tourist boards can provide lists of campsites, but check before going to a site whether there is a minimum age for camping there without an adult.

The Camping Club of Great Britain and Ireland, 11 Lower Grosvenor Place, London SW1W 0EY, has a youth section for 12–17 year olds. Until you pass a camping proficiency test you can only camp on a limited number of club sites under the guidance of a youth leader, but then you can use all the sites.

Special interest holidays

There are special interest holidays all over Britain, and the best places to get information from are the tourist boards. The British Tourist Authority, English Tourist Board and Scottish Tourist Board all produce guides to special interest holidays which include subjects as different as mountaineering and landscape painting.

Holiday adventure centres

If you don't want to specialize in one activity, there are several holidays you can go on to try a number of different things. The guides to special interest holidays published by the British Tourist Authority, English Tourist Board and Scottish Tourist Board include details of these multi-activity centres.

The Youth Hostels Association organizes adventure holidays covering a whole range of sports as well as walking. The minimum age for unaccompanied children in England and Wales is 11 and usually 14 in Scotland.

If you want a real challenge, the Outward Bound Trust, Avon House, 360 Oxford Street, London W1N 9HA, runs adventure courses for children aged 10 and over. Activities included in the courses are canoeing, orienteering, climbing, caving, sailing, camping and, for older children, full 3–4 day expeditions where you learn to survive under tough, outdoor conditions.

Pony trekking and riding

You can go pony trekking without having any riding experience. On a trek you go out in a group accompanied by a guide and an instructor, and the ponies go at walking pace.

At riding centres you get proper instruction in riding a horse (walking, trotting and cantering) and you can learn to jump and groom a horse. The following organizations have lists of riding and/or pony trekking centres:

English Riding Holiday and Trekking Association, British Horse Society, British Equestrian Centre, Kenilworth, Warwicks. CV8 2LR
Ponies of Britain (for both trekking and riding), Brookside Farm, Ascot, Berks. SL5 7LU
Association of British Riding Schools, 7 Deer Park Road, Sawtry, Huntingdon, Cambs. PE17 5TT

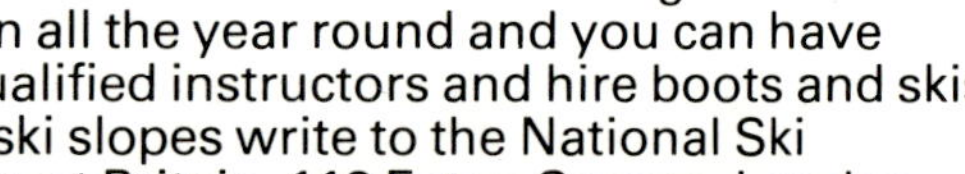

Skiing

The place to snow ski in Britain is Scotland. The season runs from December to May and there are four main centres: Aviemore in the Cairngorm Mountains, Glenshee, which is near Braemar, Glencoe, and Lecht in the eastern Cairngorms. Write to the Scottish Tourist Board for details (address on page 79).

There are also over 60 artificial ski slopes in Britain, where you can learn to ski from about the age of 7. The centres are open all the year round and you can have lessons from qualified instructors and hire boots and skis. For a list of dry ski slopes write to the National Ski Federation of Great Britain, 118 Eaton Square, London SW1W 9AF.

Archaeology

If you are interested in how people lived in the past, you might like to help explore ancient sites and record finds, before they are lost by being built over. The minimum age for helping on excavations is usually 16 though there are exceptions. The Council for British Archaeology, 112 Kennington Road, London SE11 6RE will put you in touch with your local society.

Young Rescue is an organization specially for 9–16 year olds. For information write to Dr Kate Pretty, New Hall, Cambridge CB3 0DF.

Climbing

Climbing is a difficult and often dangerous sport, and it is unusual to take it up before you have had quite a lot of experience at hill walking or without joining a club. The governing body for the sport is the British Mountaineering Council, Crawford House, Precinct Centre, Booth Street East, Manchester M13 9RZ.

Caving

This is another exciting sport that it is impossible to do safely without joining a club. The main caving areas in Britain are Derbyshire, the Northern Pennines, South Wales and the Mendip Hills. For information, write to the National Caving Association, Bethal Green, Calderbrook Road, Littleborough, Lancs.

Fishing

You can fish anywhere off the coast of Britain, provided it is safe, and sometimes you can go out on fishing trips with local fishermen. However, there are very complicated rules and regulations about fishing on inland waters and for this it is best to join a club which has its own stretch of water. Fishing tackle shops are often the best places to go to for preliminary advice and the Scottish, Welsh and Northern Ireland Tourist Boards all produce good fishing guides.

Other useful addresses:
The English International Fly Fishing Association, 94 Longdon Road, Knowle, Solihull, West Midlands B93 9HR
National Anglers' Council, 5 Cowgate, Peterborough, Cambs. PE1 1LR
Salmon and Trout Association, Fishmongers' Hall, London Bridge, London EC4R 9EL

Golf

Many golf clubs have junior members or accept visiting players, but if you are a beginner you might prefer to play on a public course. There are about 200 public courses in England and Wales where you can play if you are 8 or over. Write to the National Association of Public Golf Courses, 948 Castle Lane East, Bournemouth BH7 6SP.

The Scottish Tourist Board produces a booklet with details of about 400 courses and clubs which welcome visitors and the Northern Ireland Tourist Board will also advise you on playing golf in Ulster.

Cycling

There are two main sorts of cycling – touring and racing. If you are interested in going touring, write to the Cyclists' Touring Club, Cotterell House, 69 Meadrow, Godalming, Surrey GU7 3HS. If you are a good cyclist and want to get involved in racing, write to the British Cycling Federation, 70 Brompton Road, London SW3 1EN.

Air sports

There is a minumum age for doing most air sports. You have to be 17 for flying an aeroplane solo, and 16 for gliding, parachuting or hang gliding. Parascending is an exception and you can usually start this at about 14.

In parascending you are towed along by a landrover, or a boat, wearing an open parachute which lifts you into the air. You then let go of the tow line and come back down to the ground as though you were parachuting.

Aircraft Owners and Pilots Association, 50 Cambridge Street, London SW1
British Gliding Association and British Parachute Association, Kimberley House, 47 Vaughan Way, Leicester LE1 4SG
British Hang Gliding Association, 167a Cheddon Road, Taunton, Somerset TA2 7AH
Association of Parascending Clubs, Room 6, Exchange Buildings, 34/50 Rutland Street, Leicester

Water sports

Sailing

You don't have to own your own boat to learn to sail, or go on the open sea. There are sailing clubs all over Britain on lakes, reservoirs, and broad rivers, and most accept junior members. Write to the Royal Yachting Association, Victoria Way, Woking, Surrey GU21 1EQ for details of clubs and sailing schools.

Canoeing

Beginners canoe on quiet streams and canals before trying fast-flowing rivers or the sea. Once you know how to canoe, you can enter competitions, for example, long distance racing or rough water obstacle racing (canoe slalom). Write to the British Canoe Union, Flexel House, 45/47 High Street, Addlestone, Weybridge, Surrey KT15 1JV, or, if you are an experienced canoeist interested in going on touring trips, to the Canoe Camping Club, 12 Western Road, Aldershot, Hants.

Surfing

Surfing is riding on an incoming wave either lying or standing on a board. The best areas for the sport are off the coasts of Cornwall and South Wales, though you can surf in other areas of Britain when sea conditions are right. You can often hire boards at main surfing resorts. If you want more information, try writing to the British Surfing Association, 16/18 Bournemouth Road, Parkstone, Poole, Dorset BH14 0ES.

Windsurfing

In windsurfing you use a special type of surf board with a sail attached to it. This means you can use the wind as well as the water to move you along. You can windsurf both on inland waters and the sea. For more information write to the Windsurfer Class Association of Great Britain, c/o Windsurfer U.K. Ltd, 489 Finchley Road, London NW3 6HS.

Water skiing

Water skiing is similar to snow skiing, except that you do it on water and are towed along by a boat. Unlike surfing, it can be done on inland waters. Most clubs have their own boats and provide equipment as well as instruction. Write to the British Water Ski Federation, 70 Brompton Road, London SW3 1EG.

Skin diving

Swimming underwater is extremely strenuous. There are two main sorts of skin diving: snorkelling and "scuba" or aqualung. The snorkeller swims near the surface of the water, breathing in air through a tube, or dives as far down as he can holding his breath. The aqualung diver carries a supply of air in a bottle on his back and so can dive deeper and stay underwater longer.

Training in both sports starts in a swimming pool, or at the most in a very sheltered outdoor pool or cove, and you first have to pass a test in basic swimming and get a medical certificate to show you are fit.

The British Sub-Aqua Club is at 70 Brompton Road, London SW3 1HA. The junior section of the club, for 9–15 year olds, is the National Snorkellers' Club, 13 Langham Gardens, Wembley, Middx HA0 3RG.

General addresses:
Sports Council, 70 Brompton Road, London SW3 1EX
Scottish Sports Council, 1 St Colme Street, Edinburgh EH3 6AA
Sports Council for Wales, Sophia Gardens, Cardiff CF1 9SW
Sports Council for Northern Ireland, 49 Malone Road, Belfast BT9 6RZ

Map of Britain

This is a simple map of Britain showing you a few main towns, airports, rivers and hills. The different colours indicate different types of land and important farm and industrial products are marked by symbols. The lines of latitude and longitude show you Britain's position on the globe.

Key to colours and symbols

- Farmland
- Heath, moorland or forest
- Industrial land
- Cattle
- Sheep
- Cereals
- Fruit
- Fish
- Coal
- Gas
- Oil

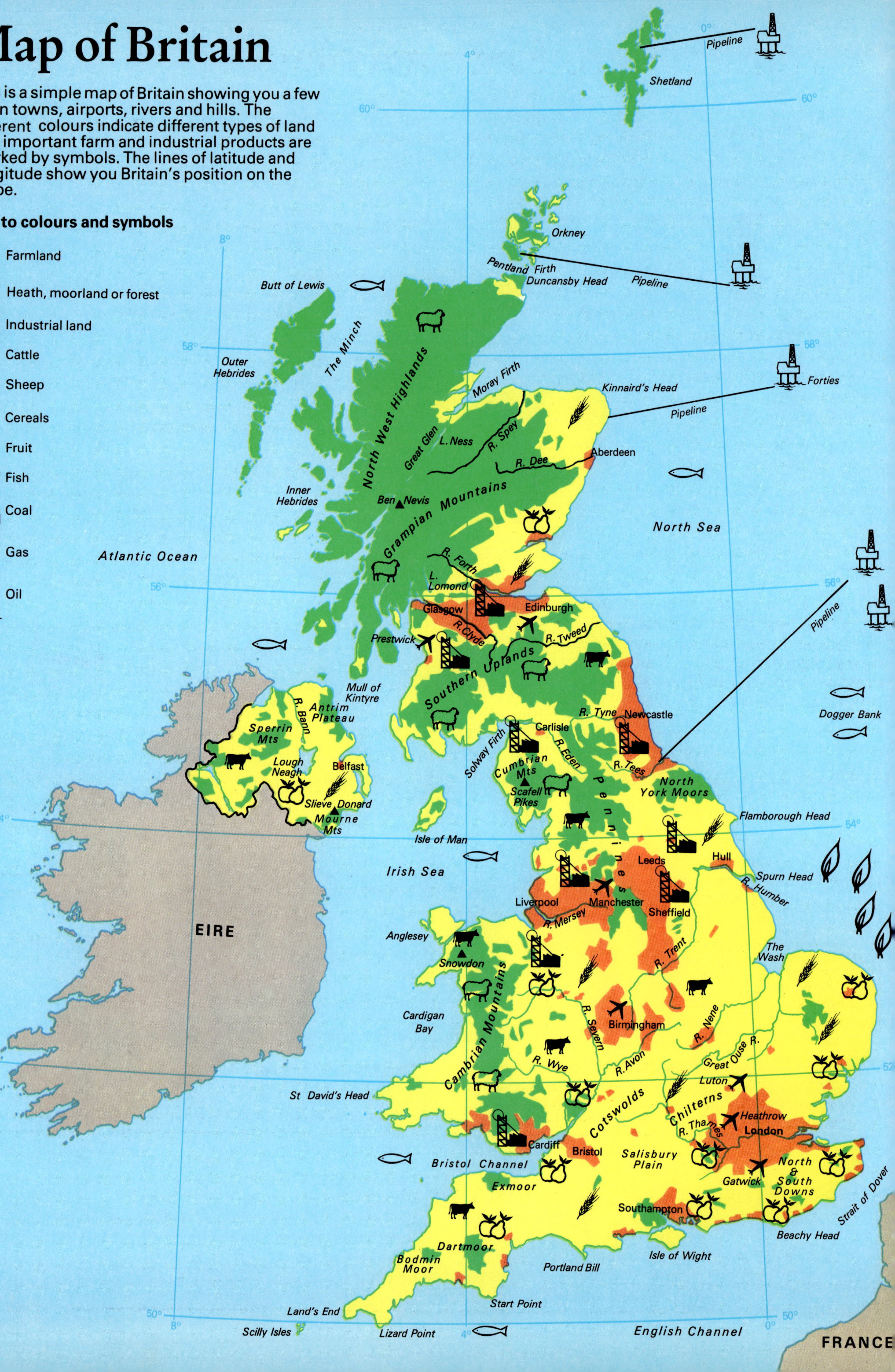

Introduction to Regional Maps

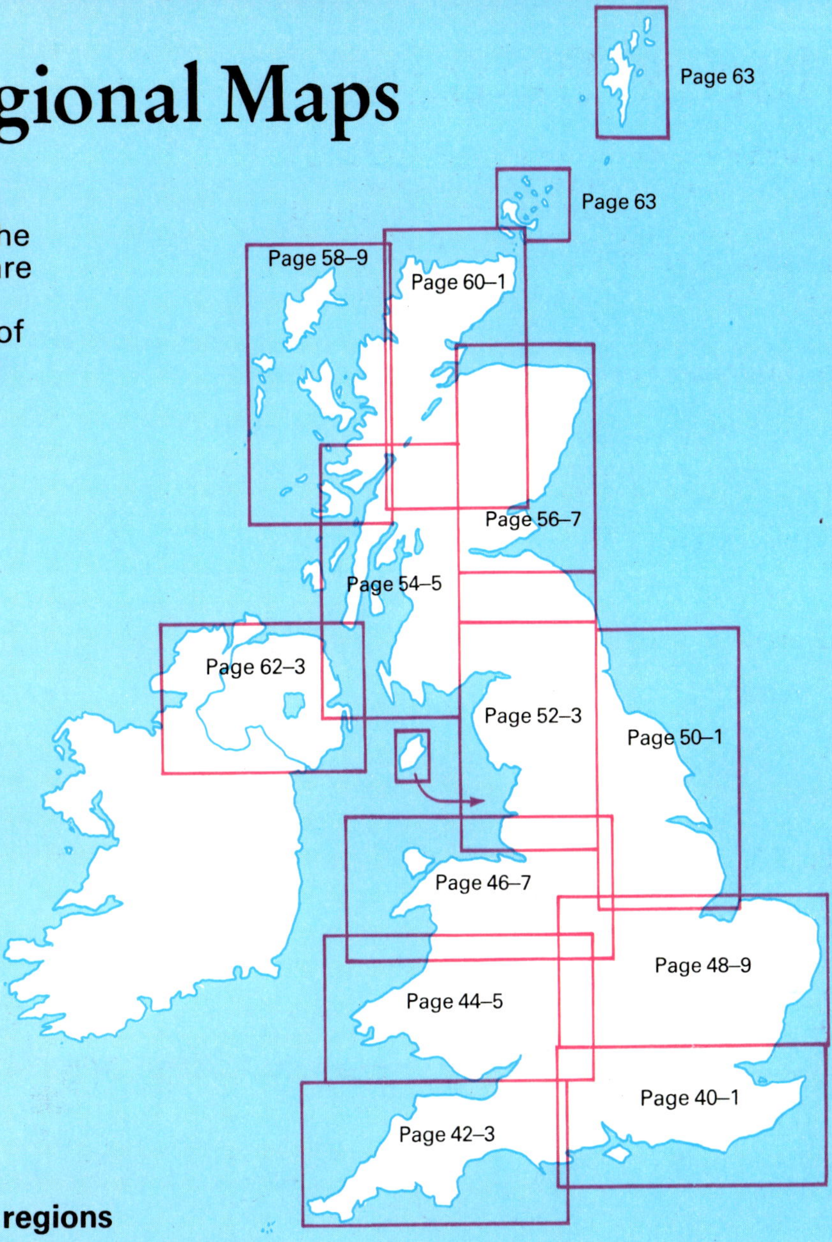

On the next 24 pages you will find 12 regional maps of Britain, which has been divided into the areas shown on this sketch map. All the maps are to the same scale and each one joins up or overlaps with the next. Notes round the edges of the maps tell you which page to turn to for the continuation, so you can easily find your way from one to the other.

The maps show large towns and built-up areas, main roads, railways, rivers, farmland, woodland, national parks, and so on. The key to the colours used on the maps is at the foot of this page.

Interesting places to visit are also shown on the maps. They are marked with symbols and most of them are named. The symbols are explained in the key below. Note, though, that the maps are not detailed enough for you to be able to use them to get from one place to another. To find the exact position of the places mentioned you will need a good road atlas and sometimes an Ordnance Survey map too.

Many of the places to visit are also mentioned in the gazetteer on page 64, or are described elsewhere in this book. If you want to find out more information about them, the national and regional tourist boards can give you details.

Key to regions

Page 40–1 South East England
Page 42–3 South West England
Page 44–5 South Wales
Page 46–7 North Wales
Page 48–9 Eastern England
Page 50–1 North East England
Page 52–3 Northern England
Page 54–5 South West Scotland
Page 56–7 Eastern Scotland
Page 58–9 North West Scotland
Page 60–1 Northern Scotland
Page 62–3 Northern Ireland
Page 63 Orkneys and Shetlands

Key to map symbols

- Cathedral or abbey
- Castle
- Historic house
- Museum
- Roman site or remains
- Prehistoric site
- Safari park
- Zoo or wildlife park
- Bird collection or sanctuary
- Nature trail
- Farm park or farm trail
- Forest
- Fun thing (e.g. model village)
- Steam railway
- Old ship
- Airport
- Ferry
- ▲ Mountain top

Key to map colours

- Built-up area
- Farmland
- National park, area of outstanding natural beauty or woodland
- Moor or heathland
- Water
- Beach
- County boundary
- Railway
- Motorway
- Other road
- Canal
- River

South East England

see page 48

see page 45

see page 43

You can look round the stables at the **Courage Shire Horse Centre** and see the blacksmith's shop.

Mapledurham is an Elizabethan mansion by the Thames. There is a watermill nearby, where corn is ground.

The Iron Age Celts may have cut this **White Horse** into the chalk hillside of the Berkshire Downs.

At **Windsor Safari Park** you can drive through reserves where there are lions, tigers, rhinos and giraffes.

Salisbury Cathedral was built in the 1200s in the Early English style. It has the tallest spire in England.

Cowes is famous for sailing. An international festival is held every August and there is a national sailing centre there.

Portchester Castle was built by the Normans inside the walls of an old shore fort originally built by the Romans.

Fishbourne is the largest Roman villa so far discovered in Britain. This is part of the mosaic stone floor.

see page 49

This is a baboon at **Broxbourne Zoo,** which is an open-air exhibition of about 250 animals.

Southend-on-Sea is one of the biggest seaside resorts in Britain. It has the longest pier in the world.

You can go on boat trips along **Regent's Canal** in London. Many go through Regent's Park to the zoo.

This is Queen Elizabeth I in the **National Portrait Gallery,** London, which runs special children's projects.

These chalk cliffs, near Eastbourne, are called the **Seven Sisters.** The dips on the top are ancient river valleys.

William the Conqueror built **Battle Abbey** to commemorate his victory over the British at the Battle of Hastings in 1066.

For several centuries the **Mermaid Inn,** at Rye, was a meeting place for notorious bands of smugglers.

The **Kent and East Sussex Railway** is an old steam railway. You can go for rides on it from Tenterden station.

South West England

Puffins nest on the cliffs at **Lundy Island.** You can take a boat trip to the island from Ilfracombe.

Tintagel is said to be the birthplace of the legendary King Arthur. There is a ruined castle on the cliff top.

The clapper bridge at **Postbridge** was probably built in the Middle Ages for packhorses carrying tin from the mines.

These steep granite cliffs meet the Atlantic Ocean at **Land's End,** which is the most westerly point of mainland England.

There is a legend that **St Michael's Mount,** in Mount's Bay, is the tip of an ancient kingdom drowned by the sea.

Wheal Martyn Museum is an open-air museum showing the history of Cornwall's clay mining industry.

At **Riverford Farm** you are taken on a guided tour in a tractor-drawn trailer and can see and touch the animals.

You can go down the caves at **Wookey Hole**. In ancient times people used to live in the caverns.

Wells Cathedral is built in the medieval Gothic style. It has about 300 statues carved on its west front.

At the **Fleet Air Arm Museum** in Yeovilton you can see naval aircraft and the original model of Concorde.

Montacute House was built in Elizabethan times. Its long gallery is the longest of that age in England.

Torquay became a popular seaside resort in the 1800s. It has such a mild climate that palm trees grow there.

The 150m high cliffs at **Sidmouth** are of old red sandstone. The sand on the beach is red too.

Abbotsbury Swannery is a collection of hundreds of swans. It was probably founded by monks in the 14th century.

In the village of **Milton Abbas** you can see many thatched cottages which are typical of the West Country.

South Wales

You can go on a steam train on the **Vale of Rheidol Railway** high up into the hills from Aberystwyth.

This cromlech at **Pentre Ifan** is the remains of a Stone Age burial chamber. "Cromlech" is Welsh for dolmen.

In the **Dan-yr-Ogof Caves** you can see weird rock formations and underground lakes.

Penscynor Wildlife Park has a good bird collection, including many parrots. These are macaws.

see page 46

St David's Cathedral is named after Wales's patron saint and St David's is the smallest cathedral city in Britain.

Pembroke Castle is built over a cavern. Its high, round keep has a roof and the gatehouse has three portcullises.

The **Brecon Beacons** got their name because signal fires used to be lit on them. From the top you can see the Bristol Channel.

Caerphilly Castle is the biggest in Wales. One tower was blasted in the 1600s and has been leaning sideways ever since.

see page 47

see page 48

see page 40

see page 43

13th century **Stokesay Castle** is a manor house which was fortified to keep out raiders from Wales.

Dudley Zoo has over a thousand animals, and some life-size models of dinosaurs. This is an orang-utan.

The oldest part of **Worcester Cathedral** is the crypt, built in 1084 for the safekeeping of saints' relics.

Sudeley Castle has interesting Tudor relics. Catherine Parr, the last of Henry VIII's six wives, lived here.

The **Welsh Folk Museum** in Cardiff has old buildings from all over Wales, including cottages, farms, a chapel and a mill.

Tintern Abbey is one of the monasteries destroyed by Henry VIII when he broke away from the Catholic Church in 1536.

The M4 motorway from England to Wales crosses the River Severn by the kilometre-long **Severn Suspension Bridge**.

Avebury Henge was built about the same time as Stonehenge. Part of Avebury village is inside the stone circle.

North Wales

At **Llandudno** you can go on the longest cable car in Britain to the top of the Great Orme headland.

Edward I made **Conwy Castle** the headquarters for his struggle against Prince Llywelyn of Wales.

This stone passage leads to the burial chamber of the prehistoric mound or "cairn" of **Bryn Celli Du.**

The **Museum of Childhood** at Menai Bridge has toys and games from the last 150 years. This is a clockwork cat.

see page 44

Caernarfon Castle is one of eight castles Edward I built in Wales in the 1200s when he was trying to conquer the country.

Snowdon is the highest mountain in England and Wales (1085m). You can sometimes see as far as Ireland from the top.

At **Gloddfa Ganol** you can go down an old mine and learn about the history of the slate mining industry in Wales.

Harlech Castle was built on a good defensive site – on a high crag by the sea, with mountains behind. It also has a moat.

see page 53

see page 51

see page 48

see page 45

Liverpool Roman Catholic Cathedral was built in the 1960s. It is round and the tower is of stained glass.

At **Knowsley Safari Park** you can drive for 8km through reserves of African animals, including cheetahs.

At the **Abbeydale Industrial Hamlet** in Sheffield you can see how steel tools were made in the 1700s.

Little Moreton Hall was built in the 1500s. You can see Tudor wood panelling and carved oak furniture.

At **Erddig Hall** you can see the servants' rooms as well as the master's, and also a laundry, bakehouse, sawmill and smithy.

Lichfield Cathedral is the only English cathedral which has three spires. They are known as the Ladies of the Vale.

There are nature trails and a woodland adventure playground in the big parklands of 17th century **Weston Park.**

Jodrell Bank is a big radio telescope which studies objects in space. There is also a small telescope that you can work.

Eastern England

Single-seater racing cars are on display in the **Donington Collection,** also vintage cars, buses and lorries.

Belvoir Castle was rebuilt in the 1800s to look like a medieval castle. Jousts are often held there.

You can learn about the history of brewing at the **Bass Museum of Brewing.** There is a model of a Victorian brewery.

Coventry Cathedral was bombed in World War II and its ruins are now joined to a modern cathedral.

see page 51

see page 47

see page 45

see page 40

This plasterwork room is in 18th century **Ragley Hall.** There is an adventure wood and a country trail in the grounds.

Today the **Grand Union Canal** is used for pleasure, but the narrow boats used to transport heavy industrial goods.

Compton Wynyates is a Tudor house. There is a minstrels' gallery, a secret staircase and a hiding hole.

There are good views from **Rockingham Castle,** which is built on top of a hill. You can see five counties.

see page 41

The **North Norfolk Railway** has historic engines and carriages. You can sometimes go on a steam train.

The **Norfolk Broads** were peat workings which flooded and became lakes. Now you can go sailing on them.

At **Grimes Graves** you can see the remains of a prehistoric flint mine which is 4,000 years old.

Ely Cathedral stands out above the flat landscape of the Fens. It has an unusual, eight-sided tower.

The deer park at **Woburn Abbey** has species from all over the world. Some, like this Père David's, are extinct in the wild.

Audley End was begun in 1603, but many rooms inside are the work of the famous 18th century designer, Robert Adam.

The **Museum of East Anglian Life** at Stowmarket has farm tools, carts and old country buildings.

You can see prehistoric and Roman relics in **Colchester Castle Museum,** which is in the keep of the Norman Castle.

North East England

At the **Darlington Railway Museum** you can see the engine *Locomotion* which pulled the world's first passenger train.

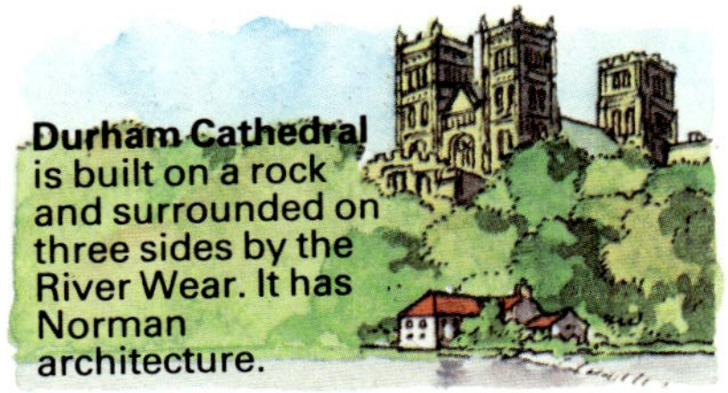

Durham Cathedral is built on a rock and surrounded on three sides by the River Wear. It has Norman architecture.

The **Washington Wildfowl Refuge** has birds from every continent. This is a hooded merganser from North America.

On **Wheeldale Moor** you can see the stone foundations of an old Roman road which used to go to Whitby.

Whitby is a historic fishing port which once had a whaling fleet. 199 steps lead to the ruined abbey on the cliff.

At **Lightwater Valley** there is an adventure playground in the style of a western fort and a western-style miniature railway.

The monks at **Fountains Abbey** traded in wool. It became one of the richest monasteries in Europe in the Middle Ages.

Castle Howard is a great house built in the 18th century in the classical style. There is a collection of historic costumes.

see page 52

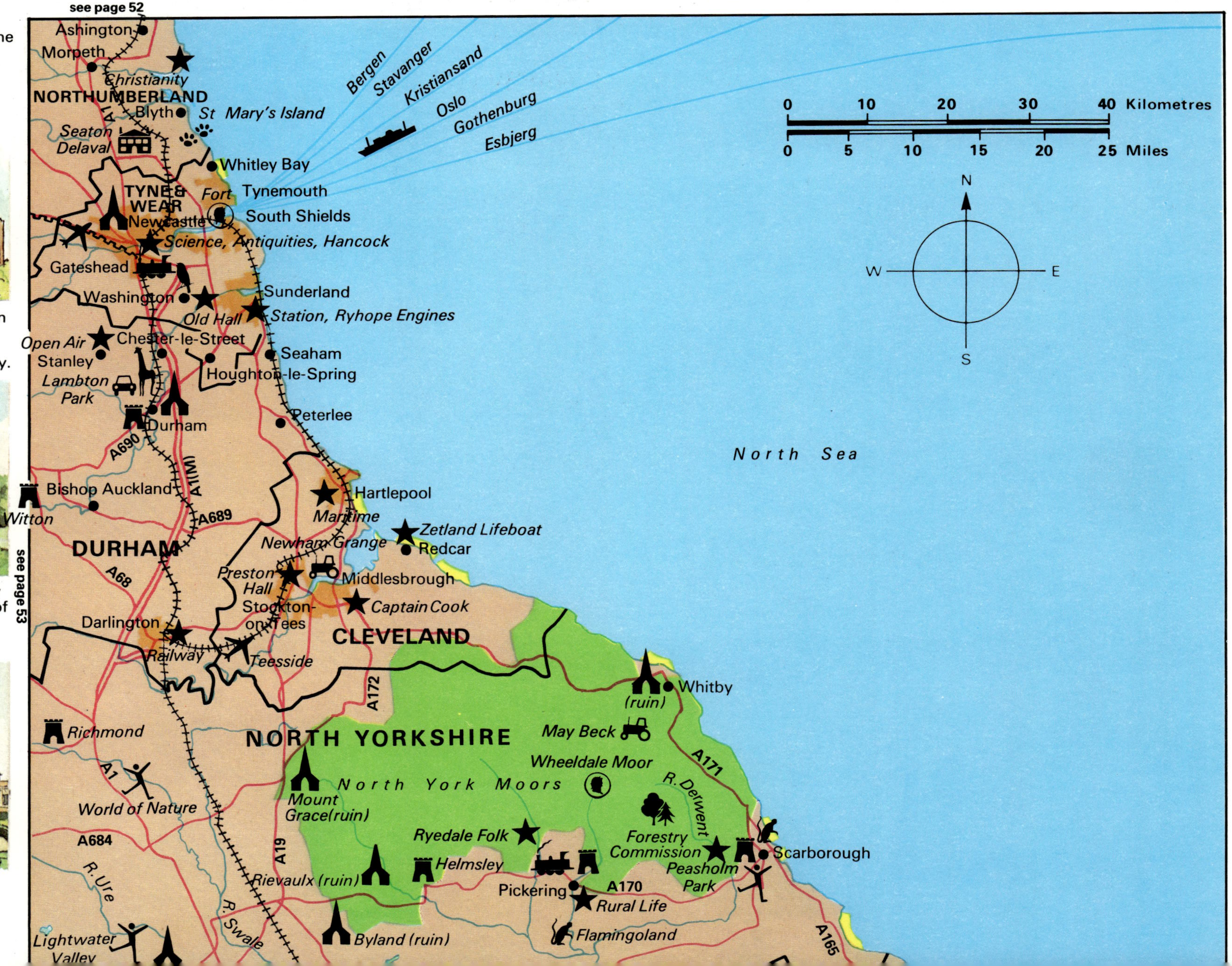

see page 53

The **Devil's Arrows** are three huge monoliths from prehistoric times. Legend says the devil shot them at a local city.

York Minster is a cathedral but has kept the Anglo-Saxon name for a large church. It has over 100 stained glass windows.

Some of the birds at **Harewood Bird Garden** are very exotic. This is a Victoria crowned pigeon from New Guinea.

In **Kirkstall Abbey Museum** there are Victorian streets of shops, houses and work places rebuilt as they used to be.

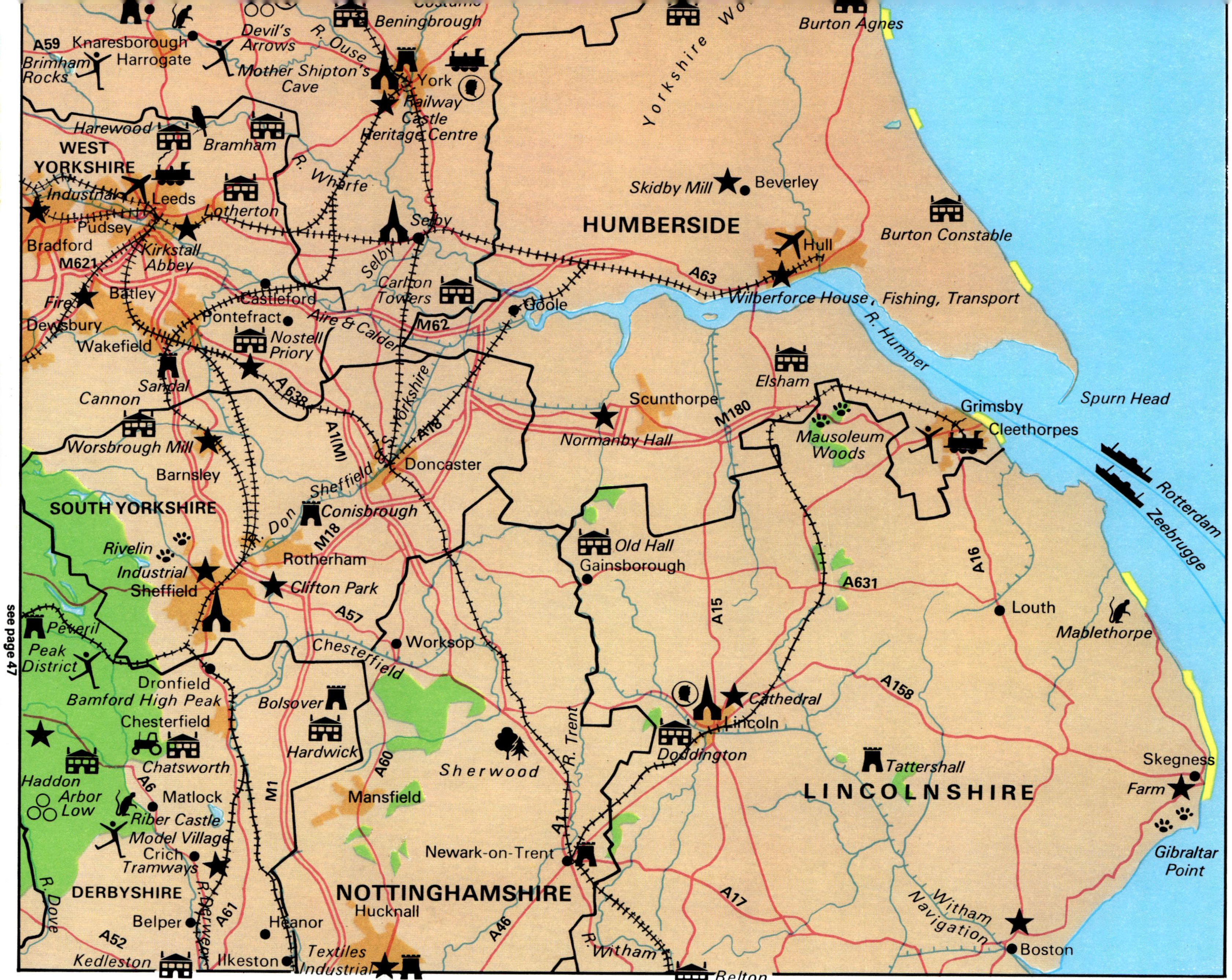

see page 47

see page 48

Conisbrough Castle has the oldest round keep in England. It was built in about 1185.

In **Chatsworth Farmyard** you can see animals from close to, watch cows being milked and horses shod.

Lincoln Cathedral is the third largest cathedral in Britain, after St Paul's and York Minster.

At Burton Constable there is a dolls' museum, a model railway and a pets' corner.

Northern England

see page 50

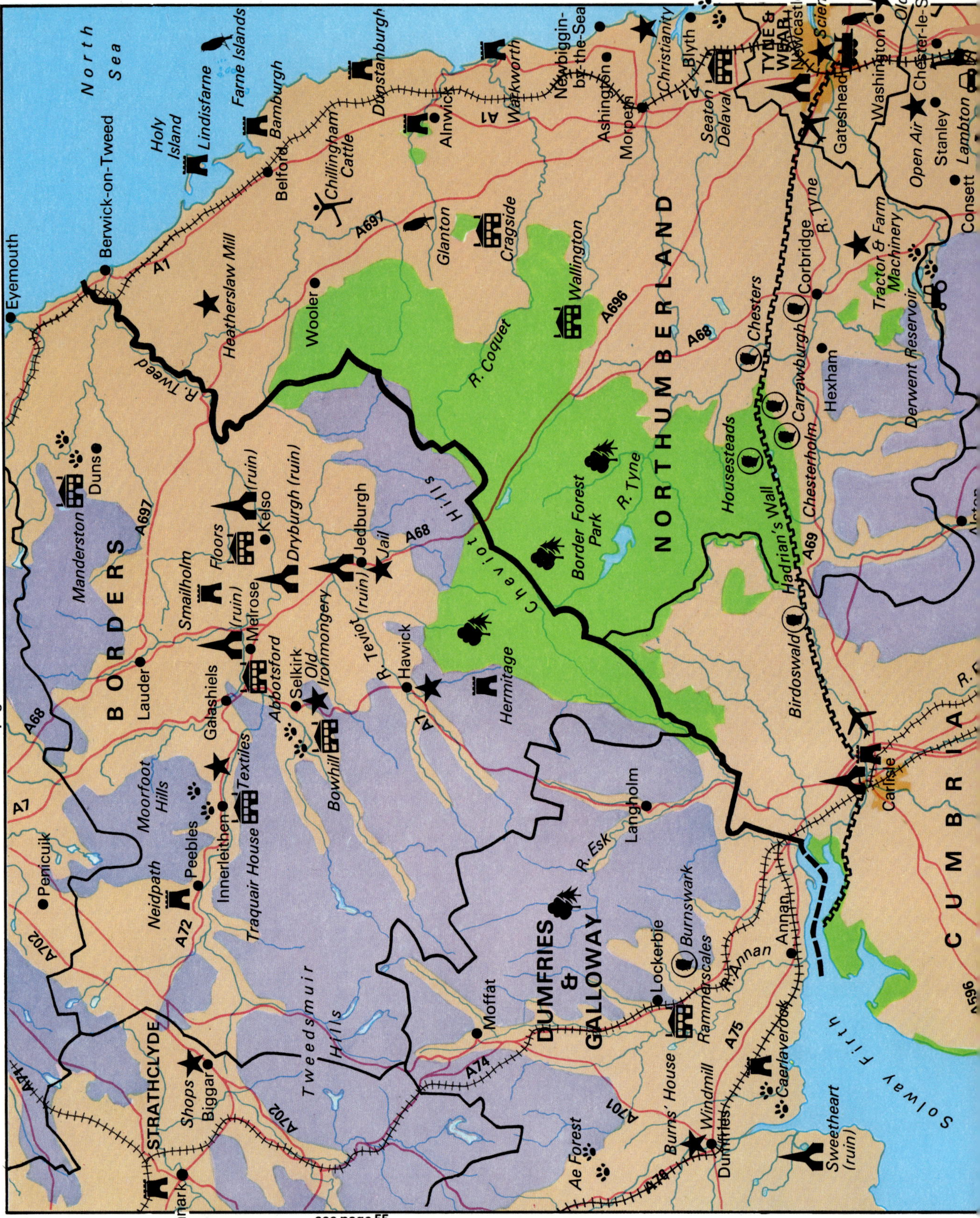

see page 57

see page 55

Statues stand on top of the huge barbican at **Alnwick Castle.** You can visit the keep, armoury and dungeon.

The **Farne Islands** are a nature reserve for seals and many different seabirds, including guillemots.

At **Gladstone Court Museum** in Biggar you can see a 19th century street with shops, a bank and a library.

Jedburgh Abbey has Norman architecture. It fell into ruins after the English burnt it during wars against the Scots.

Corbridge used to be a Roman town. This sculpture of a lion attacking another animal is in **Corbridge Roman Museum.**

Raby Castle has a great hall big enough to hold 700 knights. You can also see the medieval kitchen and servants' hall.

Scafell Pike, in the Lake District, is England's highest mountain (988m). You can see several lakes from the top.

Windermere is the biggest lake in England. It is more than 16km long and you can go for steamer and boat trips on it.

Levens Hall is an Elizabethan house with a good topiary garden. You can also see some working steam engines.

The **Lady Isabella** water wheel in the Isle of Man is the biggest in the world. It used to pump water from a lead mine.

Blackpool Tower is 160m high and you can go to the top in a lift. There is a zoo and an aquarium with a shark in it.

see page 51

see page 47

Richmond Castle is one of the oldest in Britain. You can still see the 11th century curtain walls and big keep.

Brontë Parsonage is just as it was when Charlotte, Emily and Anne Brontë, the novelists, lived there.

South West Scotland

At **Haggs Castle Museum** you can see how people have lived over the past 400 years. There are some Victorian toys.

In 1692 the Campbells massacred the Macdonalds at **Glencoe** after first spending 12 days as their guests.

Many of the animals you can see at **Blair Drummond Safari Park** are from Africa.

see page 61

There are over 250 different tartans. You can see some of them at the **Museum of Scottish Tartans** in Comrie.

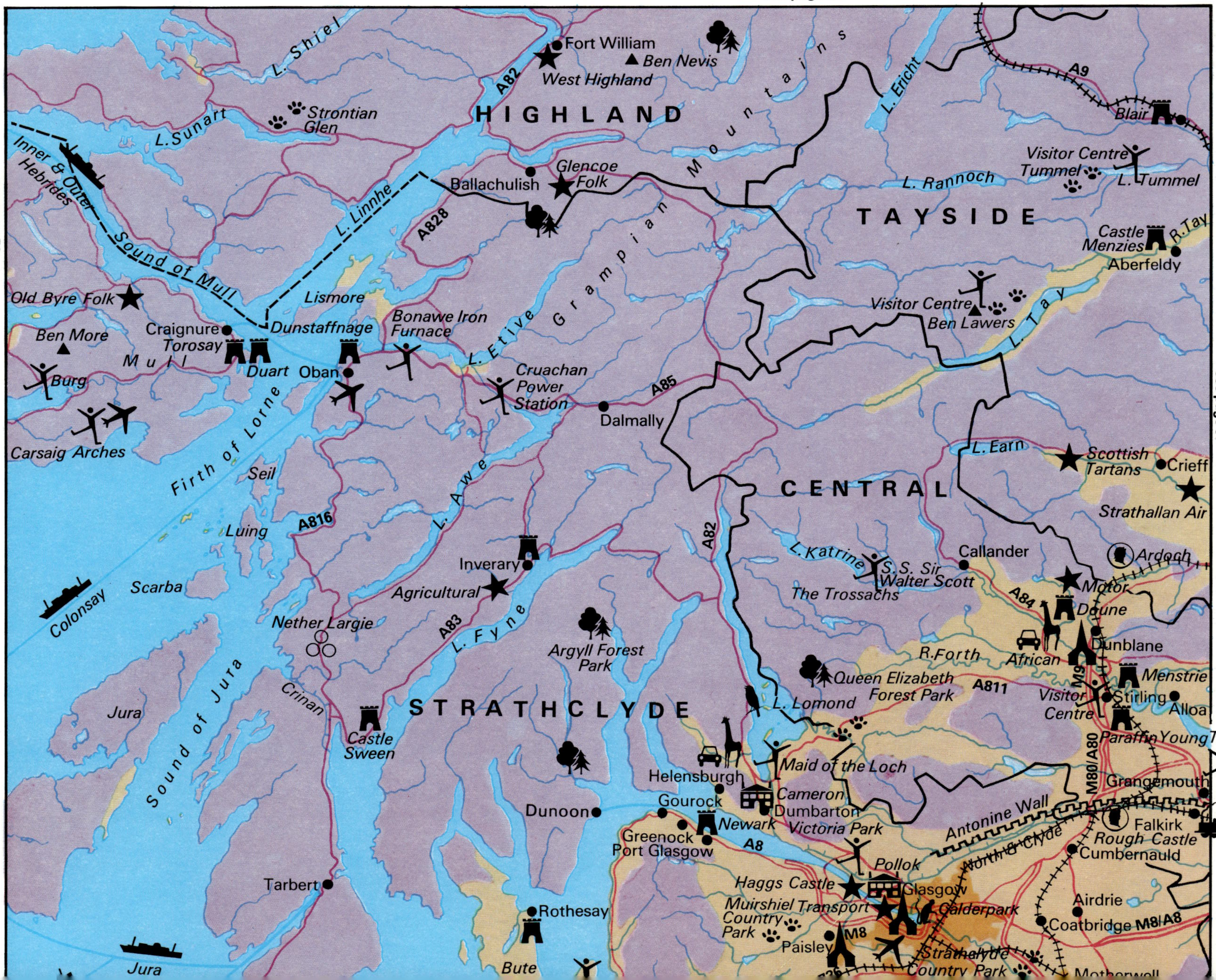

see page 57

see page 59

You can go beneath the reservoir at **Cruachan Hydro-Electric Power Station** and learn how the water makes electricity.

Inverary Castle is built in the style of a French château. You can see a good collection of old Highland weapons.

The largest Scottish loch is **Loch Lomond.** It is 40km long and in summer you can go on the paddle steamer, *Maid of the Loch.*

Stirling Castle stands on a crag. It used to be one of Scotland's royal palaces and Mary Queen of Scots was crowned here.

Glasgow Cathedral is the only complete medieval cathedral on the Scottish mainland. It is in the Gothic style.

Brodick Castle is a large, fully furnished mansion set in beautiful grounds. This is the dining room.

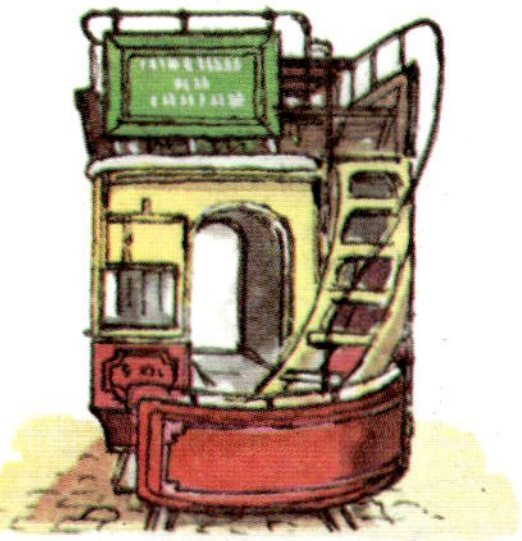

At the **Museum of Transport** in Glasgow you can see old trams, buses, cars, bicycles, railway engines and ship models.

This is the round drawing room at **Culzean Castle**, which was designed by Robert Adam in the elegant 18th century style.

see page 52

see page 63

Burns' Cottage was the childhood home of Robert Burns, poet and writer of "Auld Lang Syne". It is now a museum.

At **Cairnholy** you can see two chambered burial mounds or "cairns" from prehistoric times.

You can still see the gallows knob on **Threave Castle** where Archibald the Grim used to hang his enemies.

Lady Devorgilla founded **Sweetheart Abbey** in memory of her husband. Both are buried there.

Eastern Scotland

The 46-gun wooden frigate ***Unicorn*** was first launched in 1824. You can now go aboard it in Dundee harbour.

Glamis Castle has 9 ghosts, including that of Macbeth and a screaming monster bricked up in a secret room.

St Andrews has a ruined cathedral and castle, the oldest university in Scotland and the oldest golf course in the world.

At the **Fife Folk Museum** you can see what everyday life was like 100 years ago. This is a penny farthing bicycle.

This model of an Atholl Highlander is in **Blair Castle.** You can also see a good collection of armour.

Glenshee is a good place for skiing. You can go up the 940m Cairnwell mountain on the Glenshee chairlift.

Craigievar Castle is built in the Scottish baronial style, with corner towers and cone-shaped turrets.

Aberdeen has become the centre for Britain's oil industry. This is an oil rig supply boat in the harbour.

see page 60

see page 61

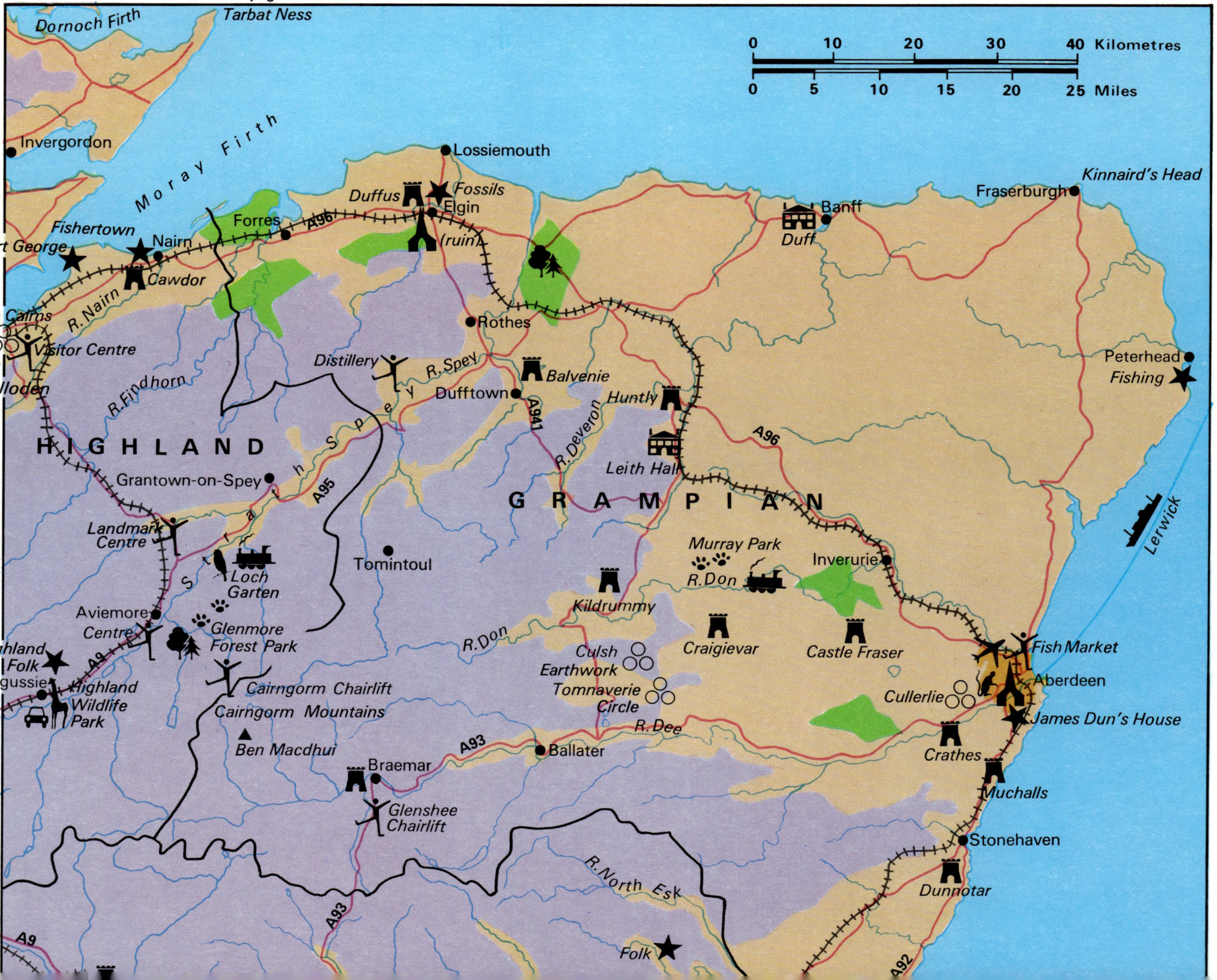

This is the king's bedchamber in 16th century **Falkland Palace**. Scottish monarchs liked to go to Falkland to hunt.

The **Forth Road Bridge** is the longest suspension bridge in Britain. It is nearly 2km long and was opened in 1964.

You can see exotic plants from all over the world at **Edinburgh Royal Botanic Gardens**. These are giant lilies.

Hopetoun House is an 18th century Adam mansion in large parklands. There is a nature trail and a rooftop viewpoint.

see page 54

see page 52

You can see old railway vehicles at the **Scottish Railway Preservation Society** in Falkirk.

The Romans built the turf rampart and ditch of the Antonine Wall. You can see remains at **Rough Castle**.

Mary Queen of Scots lived at the **Palace of Holyroodhouse**. You can see the state apartments.

You can go on a boat trip round **Bass Rock**. Its population of seabirds includes 8,000 gannets.

North West Scotland

Stornoway is the main town in the Western Isles. The Vikings launched attacks from its harbour in the 11th century.

This litre drinking horn of clan chief Rory More is in **Dunvegan Castle.** He could empty it in one go.

"Black houses" have no chimney, only a hole in the roof for the smoke. You can go inside **Skye Black House.**

Rare subtropical plants flourish in **Inverewe Gardens** because the climate is warmed by the Gulf Stream.

Beinn Eighe Nature Trail is in one of Scotland's most remote areas. You might see a rare golden eagle.

There is a legend that the Bronze Age **Callanish Standing Stones** are a circle of petrified giants.

The **Skye Cottage Museum** is in a small croft at Kilmuir. You can see Highland furniture and household and farming tools.

The Isle of Skye is dominated by the peaks of the **Cuillin Hills.** The area is good for climbing.

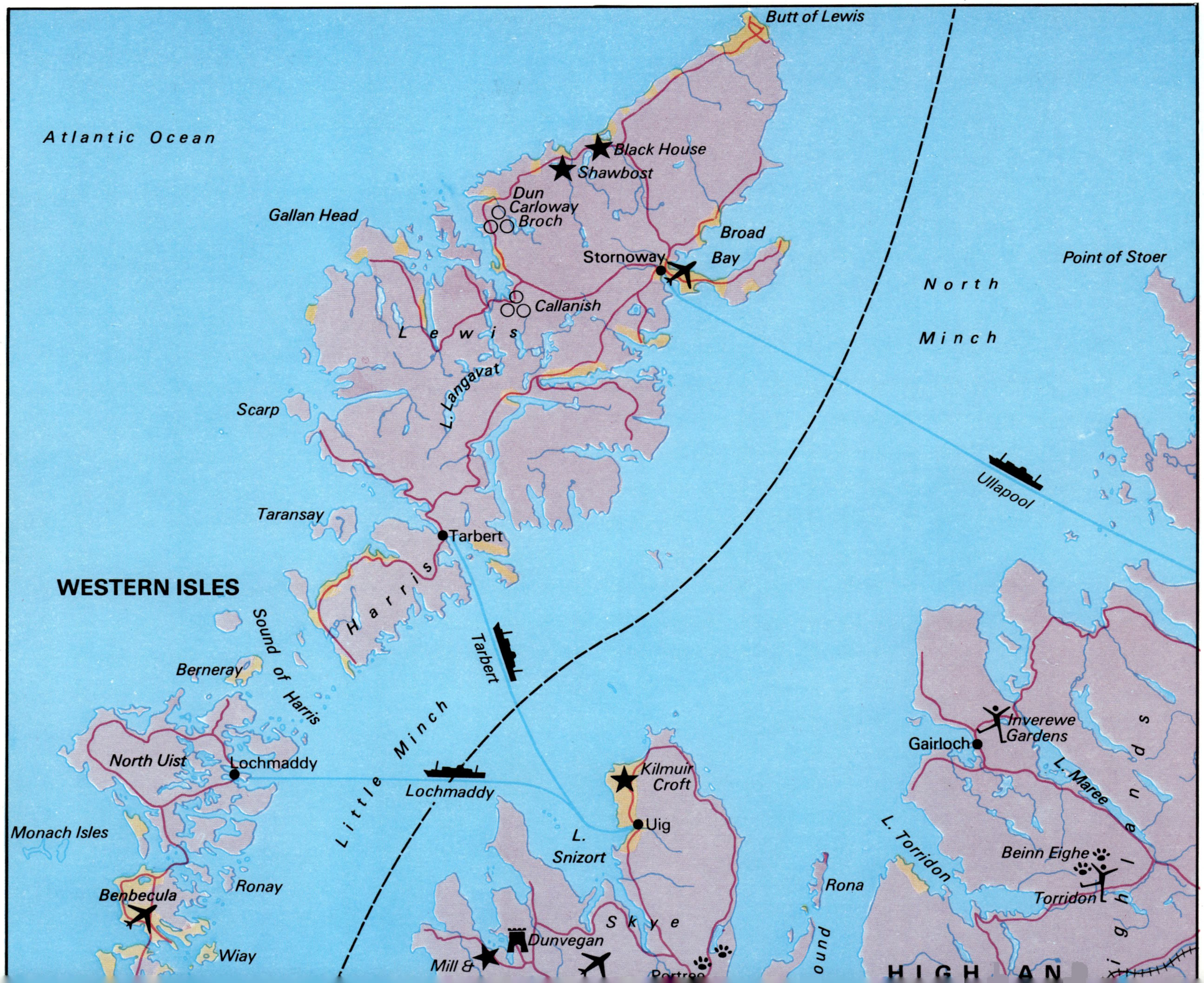

see page 60

Eilean Donan Castle **Eilean Donan Castle** was built where three lochs meet. In 1719 it was bombarded by an English warship and had to be rebuilt.

You can see two Iron Age brochs at **Dun Telve** and **Dun Troddan**. Brochs are seen nowhere but in Scotland.

Oban is a major centre in the Western Highlands. It is a tourist town, fishing port and steamer and ferry terminal.

St Mary's Abbey is on Iona. St Columba lived here when he came from Ireland to convert the Scots to Christianity in AD 563.

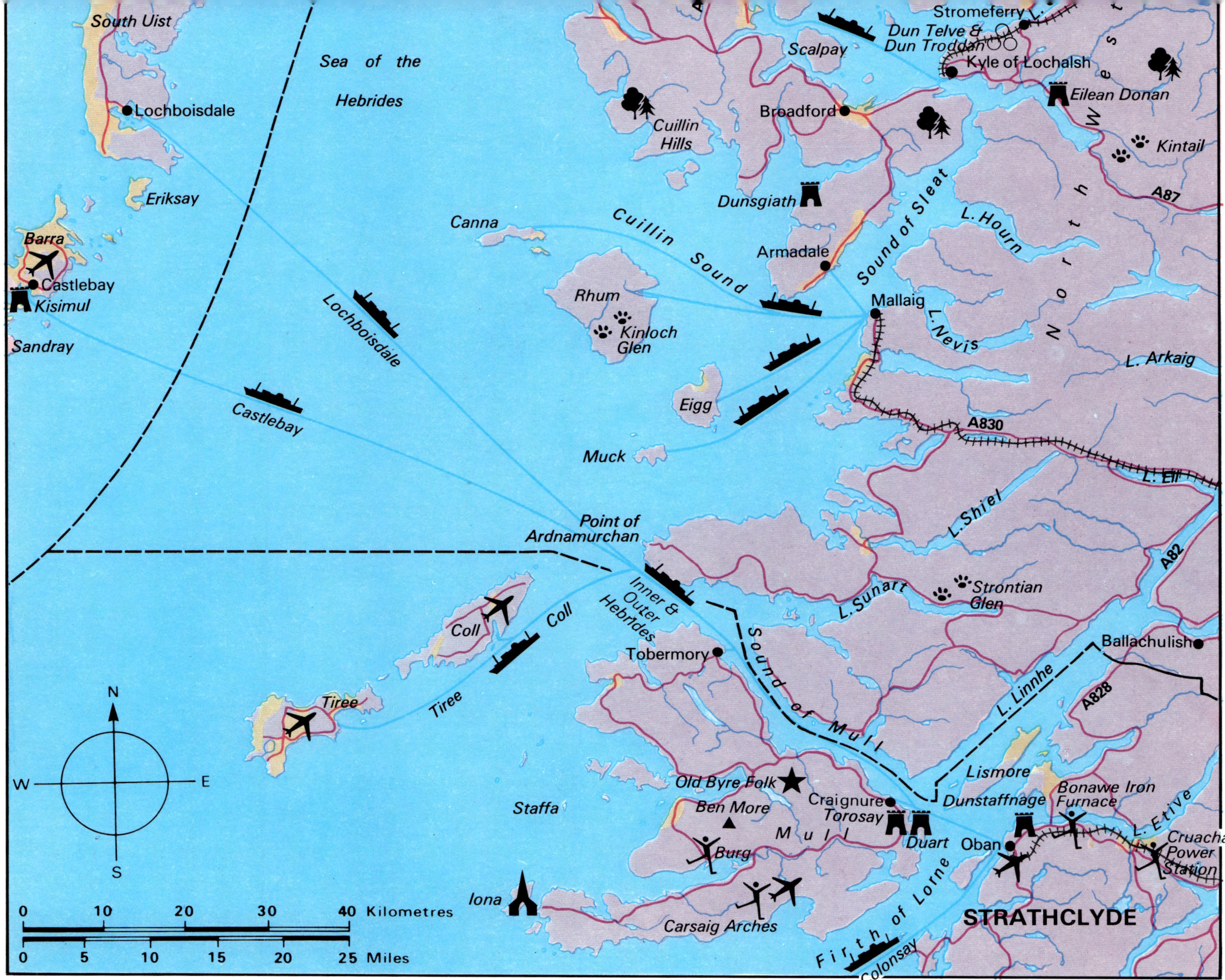

see page 61

see page 54

The owners of **Kisimul Castle** were well-known for piracy and used to seize English ships.

Loch Druidibeg nature reserve is the most important breeding ground in Britain for greylag geese.

In **Duart Castle** dungeon you can see models of prisoners from a Spanish galleon which was blown up in 1588.

The most usual way of getting to the Scottish islands is by boat. This is the ferry ***Islands of the West***.

Northern Scotland

13th century **Elgin Cathedral** used to be called the Lantern of the North because it was so beautiful.

see page 63

Dunnet Head is the most northerly point of mainland Britain. Rough seas sometimes smash the lighthouse windows.

At **Hugh Miller's Cottage** you can see some of the famous geologist's fossils. Miller was born here in 1802.

This is a clan grave at **Culloden**, where Bonnie Prince Charlie's army was routed by the English in 1746.

see page 58

Dunrobin Castle is in a great park overlooking the sea. There are paintings, furniture, tapestries and animal heads.

Fort George is one of the biggest 18th century fortresses in Europe. The English built it to suppress the Highlanders.

Inverness is one of Scotland's oldest towns. It lies on the River Ness and is often called the capital of the Highlands.

Medieval **Cawdor Castle** has a moat and a drawbridge. There are beautiful gardens and a nature trail in the grounds.

Loch Ness is famous for its monster, which has been seen near Urquhart Castle. People say it looks like a dinosaur.

You can go round **Glenfarclas Distillery** and see how Scotch whisky is made. The vapour is collected in these stills.

The **Caledonian Canal** provided a safe inland passage between the Irish and North Seas. Now it is used for pleasure.

The highest mountain in Britain is **Ben Nevis**, which towers above the town of Fort William. It is 1344m above sea level.

see page 59

see page 54

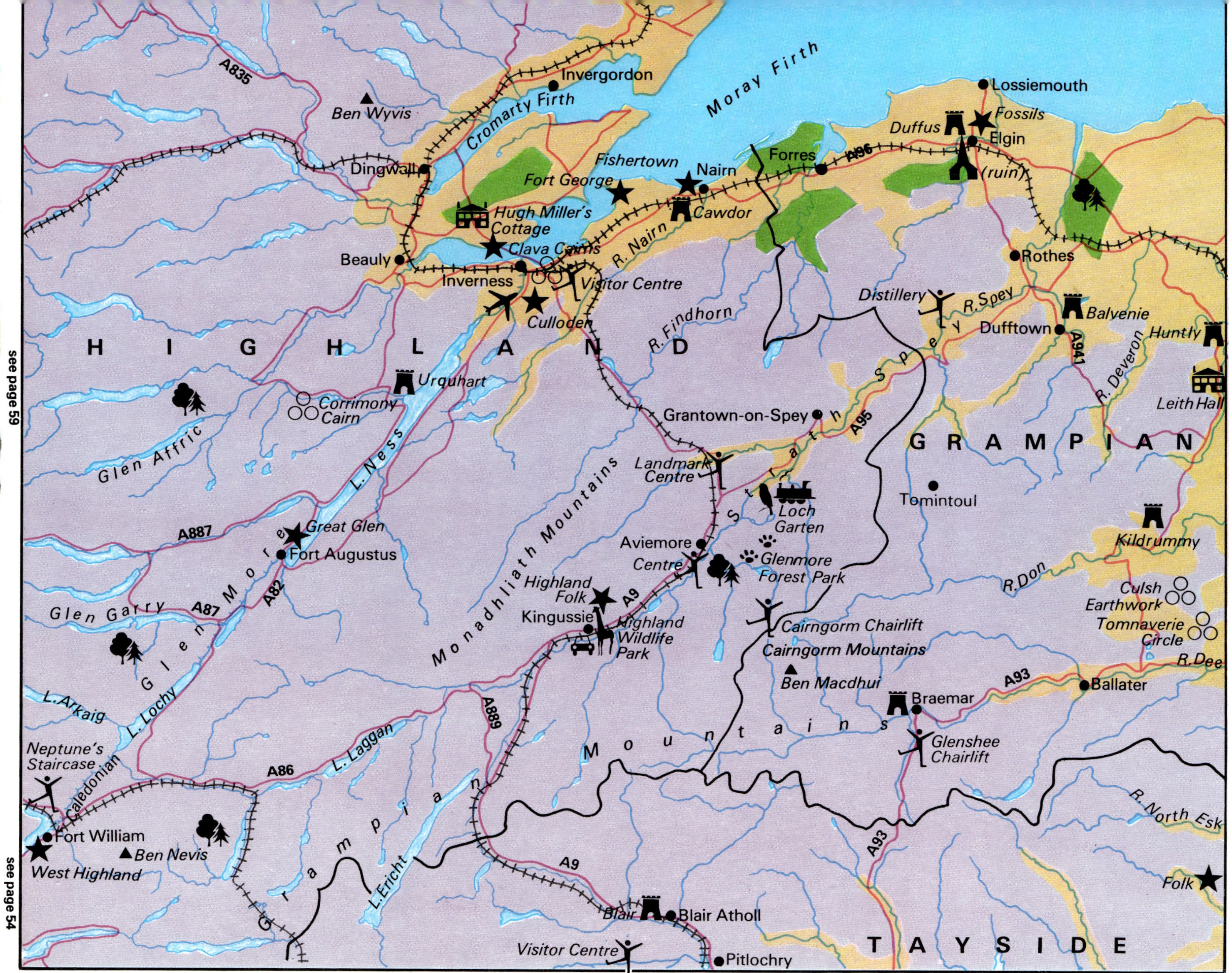

see page 56

see page 56

You can see how people lived in the past at the open-air **Highland Folk Museum.** This is nursery furniture.

Aviemore is Scotland's main winter sports resort. This is the curling rink at the **Aviemore Centre.**

The **Cairngorms** are Britain's highest mountain range. They are good for skiing and climbing.

You can walk into the pitch-black passage of an underground earth house at Iron Age **Culsh Earthworks.**

Northern Ireland

The **Giant's Causeway** is a weird formation of volcanic rock which cooled into 6-sided columns.

Dunluce Castle was abandoned after the kitchen and cooks fell into the sea in a storm. There is a big cave below.

The **Ulster American Folk Park** tells the story of the many Irish settlers in the New World from the early 1700s on.

Lough Erne has over 150 wooded islands and is good for birdwatching. There are specially good heronries.

You can see the night sky projected on the dome of the **Planetarium** at Armagh. There is also a telescope you can work.

Navan Fort was probably not used for defence, but was the palace of Queen Macha, who ruled Ulster in about 300 BC.

You can go round **Belleek Pottery** and see how the porcelain is made. It first became famous in the 1800s.

Lough Neagh is the biggest lake in Britain (400 sq km). It is good for cruising, sailing, fishing and birdwatching.

Orkneys and Shetlands

You can see remains of prehistoric, Dark Age and Viking villages at **Jarlshof.** These are Iron Age round houses.

Ferries to the Orkney Islands land at **Stromness.** There has been a harbour there since Viking times.

You can go on **Shanes Castle Railway** by the edge of Lough Neagh. There is a nature reserve too.

Carrickfergus Castle was built by the Normans. You can see armour and weapons and go down the dungeons.

Belfast is the capital of Northern Ireland. The city hall was built in 1906 and its copper dome is a landmark.

At the **Ulster Folk and Transport Museum** you can see a weaver's cottage, a spade mill, a forge, a school and a village church.

Ballycopeland Windmill is an 18th century corn grinding mill with wooden machinery. It is kept in working order.

This is the dining room at **Castle Ward,** an 18th century mansion on the shores of Strangford Lough.

Gazetteer

On the following pages are some ideas for interesting places to visit throughout Britain. They are listed under their counties (which are in alphabetical order) and under the nearest town or village. You will be able to find the approximate position of many of the places mentioned on the maps in this book, but in order to find out exactly where they are you will need a good road atlas and sometimes an Ordnance Survey map too. Before setting out to visit any of the places, always try to get in touch with the tourist office which covers that area. They will be able to give you accurate information on opening hours, admission charges, and more detailed descriptions of the places and directions on how to get to them. You will find that many places are only open in the summer months , several are closed at least one day a week and some may only be open at weekends or in the afternoons. The addresses of the tourist boards are on page 79.

ENGLAND

AVON (Map page 45)

Bath. *American Museum.* See page 31.
Bath. *Roman Baths and Pump Room.* See page 13.
Bath. *Bath Roman Museum.* Relics from the Roman baths and other sites.
Bath. *Museum of Costume.* See page 31.
Bower Ashton. *Ashton Court Estate Nature Trail.* 3½km long. Junction A369 with B3124, entrance at Clifton Lodge Gate.
Bristol. *Bristol Industrial Museum.* Transport by land, sea and air, manufacturing equipment, working model railway.
Bristol. *Bristol Zoo.* See page 30.
Bristol. *Frome Valley Nature Trail.* 4½km long. Start at Stapleton Bridge, Stapleton.
Bristol. *SS Great Britain.* 1843 early iron steamship designed by Brunel. You can go on board.
Bristol. *Wildlife Park.* British wildlife.
Chipping Sodbury. *Dodington House.* 18th century house with carriage museum in stables. Also has narrow gauge passenger railway, scale model aircraft, two nature trails and "adventureland" in gardens.
Oakhill, nr Bath. *Oakhill Manor.* Furnished mansion house. Collection of models of land, sea and air transport. Miniature railway from car park to house; picnic area in grounds.
Rode, nr Bath. *The Tropical Bird Gardens.* In grounds of Rode Manor.
Weston-super-Mare. *Steep Holm Island.* Nature reserve, 8km offshore.

BEDFORDSHIRE (Map page 48)

Biggleswade. *The Shuttleworth Collection.* See page 31.
Dunstable. *Whipsnade Park Zoo.* See page 30.
Leighton Buzzard. *Leighton Buzzard Narrow Gauge Railway.* Steam, diesel and petrol locomotives.
Luton. *Luton Hoo.* Exterior by Robert Adam 1767, interior remodelled early in 20th century. Contains pictures, furniture, tapestries, china, Russian jewels and mementoes of Russian Imperial Family. Gardens.
Stagsden. *Stagsden Bird Gardens.*
Woburn. *Woburn Abbey.* Contains paintings, furniture and silver. In the gardens are an ice house, grotto, maze and Chinese dairy.
Woburn. *Woburn Abbey Zoo Park.* See page 49.

BERKSHIRE (Map page 40)

Maidenhead. *Courage Shire Horse Centre.* See page 40.
Pangbourne. *Basildon Park.* Classical 1776 house with furniture and paintings. Garden.
Reading. *Museum of English Rural Life.* History of English countryside including farm and village life, crafts and household utensils.
Wargrave. *Dean Place Farm Trail,* Crazies Hill. 3km or 5km long. Warren Row turning off A423, between Henley and Maidenhead.
Windsor. *Royal Windsor Safari Park.* See page 40.
Windsor. *Windsor Castle.* See page 14.

BUCKINGHAMSHIRE (Map pages 40 and 48)

Beaconsfield. *Bekonscot Model Village.* See page 30.
High Wycombe. *Wycombe Chair and Local History Museum.* Includes chairs of most periods, also Buckinghamshire lace.
Middle Claydon, nr Winslow. *Claydon House.* Includes *Florence Nightingale Museum.*
Newport Pagnell. *Chicheley Hall.* Built early 1800s. Contains Classical hall, panelled rooms, hidden library, *Beatty Naval Museum.* Gardens.
Old Bradwell, nr Milton Keynes. *Bradwell Abbey Junior Trail.* ¾km long. Turn off H3 (Monks Way) on east side of railway bridge.
Olney. *Flamingo Gardens and Tropical Bird Zoo.*
Quainton, nr Aylesbury. *Quainton Railway Centre.* Collection of standard gauge engines. Steam train rides.
Stony Stratford. *Manor Farm Trail, Old Wolverton.* 2½km long. Turn off A422 on to Old Wolverton Road.
Waddesdon, nr Aylesbury. *Waddesdon Manor.* Built late 1800s. Contains furniture and paintings, lace and costumes. Aviary and deer in grounds.
West Wycombe. *West Wycombe Park.* House with decorated ceilings, frescoes, furniture, etc. Landscaped gardens with lake.
Wexham. *Langley Park Trail.* 3¼km long. Turn off A412, at Billet Lane.
Wing. *Ascott House.* Contains furniture and Oriental porcelain. Gardens include topiary sundial, water lilies and unusual trees.
Wolverton, nr Milton Keynes. *The Stacey Hill Collection of Industry and Rural Life.* Exhibition of industrial, agricultural and domestic items.
Great Linford. *Linford Wood Junior Trail.* 1½km long. Turn off H3 (Monks Way) to the south and take signposted trackway.

CAMBRIDGESHIRE (Map pages 48–49)

Bourn, nr Cambridge. *Bourn Post Mill.* Possibly the oldest post mill in England. You can go inside.
Cambridge. *Cambridge and County Folk Museum.* Agricultural and domestic exhibits, including toys from medieval to present times.
Cambridge. *Cambridge Brass Rubbing Centre, Wesley Church Library.*
Cambridge. *Fitzwilliam Museum.* Contains paintings, furniture, clocks, Egyptian collection, coins and medals.
Cambridge. *Paradise Nature Trail, Coe Fen.* 1½km long. A603 from Cambridge, first left after Newnham Roundabout, track between Barton Rd and Trumpington Rd.
Cambridge. *Sedgwick Museum of Geology.* Contains fossils from all over the world and different kinds of rocks.
Duxford, nr Cambridge. *Imperial War Museum.* In hangars dating from World War I. Has 60 historic and modern aircraft, including a model of Concorde.
Ely. *Stretham Engine.* Largest steam beam pumping engine still in working order. Display of items found in the Fens.
Linton. *Linton Zoo.*
Peakirk, nr Peterborough. *Wildfowl Trust.* Includes flamingoes and 100 different kinds of ducks, geese and swans.
Stamford (Lincs.). *Burghley House.* Elizabethan house including painted ceilings, Italian paintings, silver fireplaces and tapestries.
Thorney, nr Peterborough. *Thorney Wildlife Park.*
Wansford. *Nene Valley Steam Railway.* Collection includes European locomotives. Signal box open for inspection.
Wicken, nr Ely. *Wicken Fen Nature Trail.* 3km long. Wicken Village on A1123, follow signpost to Wicken Fen.

CHESHIRE (Map page 47)

Chester. *The British Heritage Exhibition.* History of Chester, with 3-dimensional plan of Roman, medieval and modern Chester, reconstruction of shops and streets and a brass rubbing centre.
Chester. *Grosvenor Museum.* Roman remains including Roman army display. Also art, folk life and natural history.
Chester. *Roman Amphitheatre.* Has an excavated underground chamber which is laid out as a garden with Roman pillars.
Congleton. *Little Moreton Hall.* See page 47.
Disley. *Lyme Park.* Elizabethan house, with 1720 Classical exterior. Contains furniture, tapestries and carvings. Gardens include a nature trail and deer.
Ellesmere Port. *Ellesmere Port Boat Museum.* Traditional canal boats, boatbuilding and repair tools.
Knutsford. *Tatton Park.* Furnished Georgian house. Gardens include a fernery, waterfowl, deer and a historical nature trail.
Macclesfield. *Gawsworth Hall.* Tudor box-framed manor house with pictures, sculpture, furniture and a carriage museum.
Macclesfield. *Jodrell Bank.* See page 47.
Malpas. *Cholmondeley Castle Gardens.* Gardens, farm with rare breeds of animals.
Nantwich. *Bridgemere Wildlife Park.* Birds of prey, waterfowl and British animals.
Poynton, nr Bramhall. *Poynton Farm Trail, Towers Road.* 4km long. East of A523, south of Bramhall.
Styal. *Quarry Bank Mill.* 18th century cotton mill and cottages in woodland. Exhibition of cotton industry.
Tarporley. *Beeston Castle.* Ruins of a moated castle, built in the 13th century.
Upton-by-Chester. *Chester Zoo.* Animals in outdoor enclosures, free-flight aviary, tropical house, aquarium and waterbus trips.

CLEVELAND (Map page 50)

Coulby Newham, Middlesbrough. *Newham Grange Leisure Farm.* Working farm with rare breeds of animals, farm trail, nature trail and old shops.
Hartlepool. *Maritime Museum.* Maritime history of Hartlepool, including shipbuilding, fishing and marine engineering.
Middlesbrough. *Captain Cook Birthplace Museum.* Early life and voyages of Captain Cook.
Redcar. *The Zetland Museum. Zetland* is the oldest surviving lifeboat in the world. Models, relics and pictures relating to sea rescue and the local fishing industry. Marine aquarium.
Stockton-on-Tees. *Preston Hall Museum.* Social history museum including old street and rooms, toy gallery, armoury and transport exhibits. Also park with zoo and riverside walk.

CORNWALL (Map page 42)

Bude. *Ebbingford Manor.* Cornish manor house. Walled garden and nature trail.
Calstock. *Cotehele House.* Tudor house with armour, banners and original furniture. Garden has watermill, and blacksmith and wheelwright shops. The *Maritime Museum* on the quay includes a restored barge.
Camborne. *Camborne School of Mines Museum.* Mineral and ore collections.
Camborne. *Cornish Engines, East Pool Mine.* A beam winding engine and a beam pumping engine.
Dobwalls. *Forest Railway.* Miniature model steam engines and signal system.
Gulval, nr Penzance. *Chysauster Ancient British Village.* See page 12.
Gweek, nr Helston. *Cornish Seal Sanctuary.* Five pools with about 18 seals at any one time.
Helston. *Cornwall Aero Park.* Display of all kinds of aircraft. Exhibition of aviation history from 1903 to the present day.
Helston. *Goonhilly Down Station.* Two big reflectors which receive radio signals from Earth satellites. Viewing area.
Helston. *Helston Borough Museum.* Folk museum.
Looe. *Murrayton Monkey Sanctuary.*
Lostwithiel. *Restormel Castle.* Ruins of a moated castle built about 1100.
Newlyn East, nr Penzance. *Lappa Valley Railway.*

Polperro. *Model Village.*
St Agnes. *Model Village.*

CUMBRIA (Map pages 52–53)

Ambleside. *Rydal Mount.* Poet Wordsworth's home from 1813–1850.
Appleby-in-Westmorland. *Appleby Castle.* Rare farm animals and birds in the grounds.
Bowness-on-Windermere. *Belle Isle.* Built in 1778 on the only inhabited island on Lake Windermere. Adam interior, with portraits and furniture. Nature walk in grounds. There is a boat service from Bowness Promenade.
Bowness-on-Windermere. *Windermere Steamboat Museum.* Victorian and Edwardian steamboats; sailing, speed and motor boats.
Brampton. *Sands House Curio Museum.* Includes a fairground organ, old fairground amusements, toys and postcards.
Brantwood. *Brantwood Nature Trail.* 5½km long. East side of Coniston Water.
Brockhole, Windermere. *Brockhole – Lake District National Park Centre.* Story of the Lake District from prehistoric times to the present. Gardens include a nature trail.
Cark-in-Cartmel, nr Grange-over-Sands. *Holker Hall.* 16th century house with 19th century additions. Gardens include an adventure playground and children's farm. Also of interest is the *Lakeland Motor Museum.*
Carlisle. *Eden Riverside Trail.* 6km long. Start at Eden Bridge, Bitts Park in Carlisle.
Castlerigg. *Castlerigg Stone Circle.* Almost complete Bronze Age circle, 30m across.
Eskdale. *Hardknott Castle.* Remains of a Roman fort.
Grasmere. *The Wordsworth Museum, Dove Cottage.* Home of poet Wordsworth from 1799 to 1808.
Hawkshead. *Grizedale Forest Visitor and Wildlife Centre.* Rocks, soils, wildlife, industrial archaeology. Nature trails.
Kendal. *Levens Hall.* See page 53.
Kendal. *Museum of Lakeland Life and Industry, Abbot Hall.* Housed in 18th century stables. Old rooms, farm section, costumes and toys, local trade and industry.
Kendal. *Serpentine Woods Nature Trail.* 1½km long. Starting point in Serpentine Road.
Keswick. *Friars Crag Nature Trail.* 2½km long. Starting point is at the municipal car park.
Lakeside – Haverthwaite, nr Newby Bridge. *Lakeside and Haverthwaite Railway.* Standard gauge railway. The station at Lakeside connects with the Windermere steamers.
Millom. *Millom Folk Museum.* Full-scale reconstruction of a passage in an iron ore mine, miner's cottage kitchen and blacksmith's forge. Also display of agricultural material.
Penrith. *Dalemain.* Medieval, Elizabethan and Georgian house. Countryside museum and deer park.
Penrith. *Hutton-in-the-Forest.* Built in the 14th century, with later additions. Contents include furniture, armour, tapestries, paintings, plasterwork ceilings and carvings. In the gardens are lakes, woods and a dovecote.
Penrith. *Lowther Wildlife Country Park.* Deer, cattle, goats, sheep, aviaries, black swans and flamingoes.
Ravenglass. *Muncaster Castle.* Built mainly in the 14th century. Inside you can see pictures, tapestries and china, furniture and a library of 6,000 books. The gardens include a tree trail, nature trail and bird gardens.
Ravenglass–Dalegarth. *Ravenglass and Eskdale Railway.* Narrow gauge railway. Also the *Ravenglass Railway Museum.*
Wast Water. *Nether Wasdale Nature Trail.* 5½km long. At the southern end of Wast Water.

DERBYSHIRE (Map pages 47, 48 and 51)

Ashbourne. *Hamilton House Toy Museum.* Collections of antique dolls, toy trains, model railways, constructional toys (including working Meccano models) and tin toys.
Attenborough, nr Long Eaton. *Attenborough Nature Reserve and River Trent.* 4km or 11km long. Take the A453 from Attenborough, and follow the signposts to the Nature Reserve.
Bakewell. *Chatsworth.* Built about 1700. You can see the state rooms, a sculpture gallery and collections of books, pictures, furniture and domestic relics. The gardens by Capability Brown include lakes and fountains.
Bakewell. *Chatsworth Farmyard.* See page 51.
Bakewell. *Haddon Hall.* Medieval manor house with banqueting hall and long gallery. Terraced rose gardens.
Bakewell. *The Old House Museum.* Includes 19th century costumes, Victorian kitchen, toys, cameras, tools and local historical items.
Bradwell, nr Hathersage. *Bagshawe Caverns.* Waterworn passage with fossils, stalagmites and stalactites.
Castleton, nr Hathersage. *Peak Cavern.* Large natural cavern with 400-year-old rope walks.
Crich, nr Matlock. *The Tramway Museum.* See page 31.
Dale Abbey, Ilkeston. *The Cat and Fiddle Mill.* 4-sail, wooden post mill built in 1788. In working order.
Derby. *Derby City Museum and Art Gallery.* Exhibitions include costumes, coins and medals, working scale model of the Midland Railway, toy and model theatres.
Derby. *Derby Industrial Museum.* Rolls-Royce collection of historic aero-engines plus the industrial history of Derbyshire.
Dinting, nr Glossop. *Dinting Railway Centre.* Steam museum, with 13 working locomotives.
Doe Lea, nr Chesterfield. *Hardwick Hall.* Elizabethan house with furniture, tapestries, portraits and needlework. Gardens include a nature walk.
Elvaston, nr Derby. *Elvaston Castle Country Park.* Parklands with lakeside nature trail, and *Elvaston Castle Countryside Museum.*
Kedleston, Derby. *Kedleston Hall.* Robert Adam house built about 1760. Contains a marble hall, furnished state rooms and an *Indian Museum* with silver and ivory collections.
Matlock. *Heights of Abraham.* Large area of woodland including the *Great Rutland Cavern* which you can walk through.
Matlock. *Riber Castle Wildlife Park, Riber Castle.* European birds and animals, including lynx, rare farm animals and butterflies. There is also a model railway and a car museum.
Matlock Bath. Gulliver's Kingdom. Miniature models of many well-known buildings from all over the world. There is a nature trail in the grounds, and an adventure playground.
Sudbury, Derby. *Sudbury Hall Museum of Childhood.*
Via Gellia, nr Cromford. *Good Luck Lead Mine.* An underground lead-mining museum.

DEVON (Map pages 42–43)

Appledore. *North Devon Maritime Museum.*
Babbacombe, Torquay. *Model Village.*
Barnstaple. *Arlington Court.* The house includes collections of shells, pewter and model ships. There is a display of horse-drawn vehicles in the stables. Victorian formal garden.
Bickleigh, nr Tiverton. *Bickleigh Castle.* Has an armoury, great hall, etc. Moated gardens.
Bickleigh, nr Tiverton. *Bickleigh Mill Craft Centre and Farm.* A restored working watermill and a farm worked by traditional methods.
Bovey Tracey, nr Newton Abbot. *Yarner Wood Woodland Walk and Nature Trail.* 2½km and 5¼km long. Start at car park at Yarner Wood National Nature Reserve.
Bridgerule, nr Holsworthy. *Furze Farm Park.* Farm animals, including rare breeds, plus donkey and waggon rides, steam engines and nature trails.
Buckfastleigh – Totnes-Riverside. *Dart Valley Railway.* 11km-long steam train ride.
Budleigh Salterton. *Bicton Gardens.* 18th century garden with tropical/cacti house, countryside museum and woodland railway.
Cowley Wood, Parracombe. *Cowley Cleave Nature Trail.* ½km long. Off A399 between Ilfracombe and Blackmore Gate. Start at Cowley Wood car park.
Dartmouth. *Newcomen Engine House.* One of the first steam engines, built by Newcomen, and still in working order.
Drewsteignton, nr Chagford. *Castle Drogo.* Built early this century. Terraced garden and walks.
Dunsford, nr Exeter. *Dunsford Nature Trail.* Up to 6½km long. Start at Steps Bridge, near Dunsford on the B3212, west of Exeter.
Exeter. *Exeter Maritime Museum.* See page 31.
Exeter. *Killerton House and Gardens.* 18th century house with a collection of costumes. Hillside gardens.
Morwellham, nr Tavistock. *Morwellham Open Air Museum.* Exhibits of local history, tramway ride into an old copper mine and woodland trails.
Okehampton. *Pinevalley Wildlife Park.* Natural environment for eagles, pelicans, vultures and other birds. Also donkeys and sheep.
Paignton. *Paignton Zoo and Botanical Gardens.*
Paignton—Kingswear. *Torbay Steam Railway.* Great Western Railway steam train rides.
Plymouth. *Buckland Abbey.* Displays associated with explorer Sir Francis Drake plus ships' models, folk gallery and medieval barn.
Plymouth. *Plymouth Aquarium.*
Plympton, nr Plymouth. *Saltram House.* George II house incorporating an old Tudor mansion. There are two Robert Adam rooms plus furniture, pictures, a kitchen and park.
Salcombe. *Sharpitor.* A museum including ships and shipbulding displays, plus 19th century photographs, old agricultural tools, dolls and dolls' furniture. Gardens.
Shebbear. *Alscott Farm Agricultural Museum.* Tractors, ploughs and other farm equipment.
Sparkwell, nr Plymouth. *Dartmouth Wildlife Park.* Includes wildlife from Britain and Europe.
Tiverton. *Tiverton Castle.* Norman fortress including a clock collection.
Torcross, nr Kingsbridge. *Slapton Sands Nature Trail.* 5km long. Turn off A379 at north end of Slapton Sands, and start at Strete Gate.
Torquay. *Kent's Cavern.* Caves which were inhabited in prehistoric times.
Totnes. *Devonshire Collection of Period Costume.*
Totnes. *Riverford Farm.* See page 42. Advance booking is essential.

DORSET (Map pages 40 and 43)

Beaminster. *Parnham House.* Tudor manor house with a museum of woodcraft. The gardens include riverside walks.
Bournemouth–Poole. *Compton Acres.* Seven different gardens, including Japanese, rock and water, and Italian.
Bovington Camp, nr Wool. *The Tank Museum.* Over 140 tanks and armoured cars.
Brownsea Island. *Brownsea Island Nature Reserve.* Take a boat from Poole Quay. The birds include herons and terns. There is a nature trail.
Cerne Abbas. *Cerne Giant.* Huge figure cut into the chalk hillside.
Christchurch, Bournemouth. *Tucktonia.* Model landscape, plus leisure complex including go-kart circuit, go-boats and pitch and putt.
Corfe. *Corfe Castle.* Ruins of a castle built in 1280.
Dorchester. *Dorset County Museum.* Includes finds from the Iron Age fort at Maiden Castle, and the study of Dorset novelist, Thomas Hardy.
Dorchester. *Maiden Castle.* See page 12.
Kimmeridge. *Smedmore.* 17th and 18th century manor house with Dutch marquetry furniture, antique dolls, and walled gardens.
Milton Abbas. *Brewery Farm Museum.* Local Dorset brewing, farming and village relics.
Puddletown, nr Dorchester. *Athelhampton.* 15th century house with great hall, Tudor great chamber, wine cellar, state bedroom and thatched stables. Gardens.
Sherborne. *Sherborne Castle.* 16th century mansion house including furniture, porcelain and pictures. Grounds by Capability Brown.
Sherborne. *Worldwide Butterflies, Compton House.* See page 31.
Wimborne Minster. *Wimborne Model Town.*

CO. DURHAM (Map pages 50, and 52–53)

Barnard Castle. *The Bowes Museum.* Includes paintings, furniture, costumes, music and children's galleries, local history and archaeology.
Beamish, nr Chester-le-Street. *North of England Open Air Museum.* See page 31.
Chester-le-Street. *Lambton Pleasure Park.* Drive through safari park and walkabout area, with adventure playground and miniature train.
Darlington. *Darlington North Road Station Railway Museum.* See page 50.
Durham. *Durham Castle.* Built about 1070.
Durham. *Durham Cathedral.* See page 50.

Shilton. *Timothy Hackworth's Cottage Museum.* Restored home, workshop and engine shed illustrate the life and work of this steam locomotive pioneer.
Shotley Bridge to Rowlands Gill. *Derwent Walk (Farming).* 10½km long. On B6310, east of Shotley Bridge, start at site of former railway station.
Staindrop, Darlington. *Raby Castle.* See page 52.

EAST SUSSEX (Map page 41)

Alfriston. *Drusillas.* Zoo park with monkeys, birds and rare breeds of cattle. There is also a pottery, miniature railway and farm playground.
Ardingly. *Wakehurst Place Gardens.* Ponds, lakes, exotic plants, shrubs and trees.
Battle. *Battle Museum.* Diorama of the Battle of Hastings and a reproduction of the Bayeux Tapestry. There are also Roman remains.
Brighton. *Brighton Aquarium and Dolphinarium.*
Brighton. *Dolls in Wonderland.* Collection of antique toys and dolls.
Brighton. *Royal Pavilion.* See page 18.
Burwash. *Bateman's.* Home of author, Rudyard Kipling. His study is kept as it was. Restored working watermill and gardens.
Ditchling. *Ditchling Common Country Park Trail.* 4km long. Off B2112 Ditchling to Haywards Heath road.
Eastbourne. *Royal National Lifeboat Institute Museum.* All types of lifeboats from earliest to present day.
Eastbourne. *Tower 73.* Display about Martello towers housed in a restored Martello tower.
Exeat, nr Seaford. *Seven Sisters Country Park Trail.* 2½km and 5km long. On A259 Eastbourne to Seaford road at Exeat Bridge over River Cuckmere.
Forest Row. *The Spring Hill Wildfowl Park.* Large grounds with rare geese, swans, cranes, ducks and other birds.
Hailsham. *Michelham Priory.* 13th century priory surrounded by moat. Contains furniture, tapestries, musical instruments and stained glass. Also has forge, wheelwright's museum and a restored working medieval watermill.
Halland, nr Lewes. *Bentley Wildfowl.* Over 100 species of bird, including swans, geese, cranes, peacocks, flamingoes and ornamental pheasants. Woodland walk.
Heathfield. *Heathfield Wildlife Park.* Free-roaming and caged animals. There is also a motor museum, "fun train" and pets' corner.
Horsted Keynes–Sheffield Park, nr Uckfield. *Bluebell Railway.* 8km long. Vintage and British Rail steam trains.
Hove. *Brighton and Hove Engineerium.* Steam museum with full-size and model engines as well as household and cooking machines.
Lewes. *Anne of Cleves' House.* Museum of local history with household equipment, furniture, Sussex ironwork and pottery.
Rottingdean. *Grange Art Gallery and Museum.* Toy collection and letters, books and illustrations by author, Rudyard Kipling.
Rye. *Model Son et Lumière.* A scale model of Rye with special lighting, music and voices telling the history of the town.
Rye. *Rye Museum.* Includes toys and dolls.
Sedlescombe. *Norton's Farm Trail.* 5km north of Hastings on A21. 3km long.

ESSEX (Map pages 41 and 49)

Colchester. *Colchester Castle Museum.* See page 49.
Colchester. *Colchester Zoo and Aquarium.* Also model railway and exhibition of old cycles.
Colchester. *Grandad's Photography Museum.* Collection of cameras and old photos. Studio takes instant Edwardian-style photos of visitors.
Dedham. *Vale of Dedham Heavy Horse Centre.* Parades of punches and shire horses. Blacksmith's shop gives demonstrations.
Halstead. *Gosfield Hall.* Has an old well and pump house.
Harlow. *Harlow Farm/Urban Trail.* 4½km or 10½km long. Start at Harlow Museum.
Harwich. *Harwich Redoubt.* Fort built in 1808 as coastal defence against Napoleon. Includes a moat, cells, cannons and museum of local finds.
Saffron Walden. *Audley End House.* See page 49.
Southend-on-Sea. *Historic Aircraft Museum.*
Tilbury. *Thurrock Riverside Museum.* History of local River Thames and surrounding area from prehistoric to recent times.
Upminster, nr Romford. *Upminster Mill.* Smock mill built in 1803 still with its original machinery. Guided tours.
Widdington. *Mole Hall Wildlife Park.*

GLOUCESTERSHIRE (Map page 45)

Ashchurch, nr Tewkesbury. *Dowty Railway Preservation Society.* Has steam locomotives, rolling stock, signalling equipment from Britain and overseas.
Berkeley. *Berkeley Castle.* Contains furniture, paintings and silver. Deer park.
Bourton-on-the-Water. *Birdland Zoo Garden.*
Bourton-on-the-Water. *Bourton Motor Museum.* 30 cars and motorcycles. Large collection of old advertising signs.
Bourton-on-the-Water. *The Butterfly Collection.* Live butterflies in glass-fronted flight cages.
Charlton Abbots. *Belas Knap Long Barrow.* 55m long barrow with three burial chambers.
Chedworth. *Denfurlong Farm Trail.* 3¼km long. Turn off A429 to Chedworth. Route is also signposted from Withington, off A435 or A436.
Cheltenham. *Cotswold Farm Park.* Rare breeds of British farm animals, farm trail, pets' corner and adventure playground.
Chipping Campden. *Chipping Campden Car Collection.* Sports cars from 1927 to 1963.
Chipping Campden. *Woolstaplers Hall Museum.* Includes early photographic/cinematographic collections, dentists' instruments and sewing machines.
Cirencester. *Corinium Museum.* Fine collection of Roman antiquities. Also reconstructions of scenes from Cotswold life.
Coleford. *Clearwell Castle.* 18th century Gothic-style house with garden and bird park.
Coleford. *Clearwell Caves Ancient Iron Mines.* Iron was first mined here over 3,000 years ago. Now you can see geological samples and displays of mining equipment.
Gloucester. *Bishop Hooper's Lodging.* 3 box-framed Tudor buildings with an exhibition of old crafts and country industries.
Gloucester. *Gloucester Brass Rubbing Centre, Gloucester Cathedral.*
Gloucester. *Prinknash Bird Park.*
Kemble, nr Cirencester. *The Clement Collection.* Includes old farming tools, carts, and butter and cheese making equipment.
Lydney. *Norchard Steam Centre.* Includes steam locomotives and steam cranes. You can go for rides on "steam days".
Newent. *The Birds of Prey Conservation and Falconry Centre.* See page 31.
Slimbridge. *The Wildfowl Trust.* See page 31.
Snowshill, nr Broadway. *Snowshill Manor.* Tudor house including toys, clocks, musical instruments, bicycles and armour.
Winchcombe. *Sudeley Castle.* See page 45.
Yanworth. *Chedworth Roman Villa.* Remains of Roman villa with baths and mosaic floors. Museum of finds from the site.

GREATER MANCHESTER (Map page 47)

Bolton. *Smithills Hall Nature Trail.* 2½km long. Start at Smithills Hall Museum in Bolton.
Bolton. *Textile Machinery Museum.*
Bramhall, nr Stockport. *Bramall Hall.* Box-framed medieval manor house in parkland with lakes and nature walks.
Bury. *East Lancashire Railway Preservation Society.* Steam and other engines and steam rides.
Compstall. *Etherow Country Park Nature Trail.* 2½km long. B6104 into Compstall.
Eccles. *Monks Hall Museum.* Contains industrial machines, toys and crafts.
Manchester. *Belle Vue Leisure Park.* Amusement park with stock cars and speedway.
Manchester. *North Western Museum of Science and Industry.* Display on cotton industry, steam power, papermaking, printing and photography, including machines, some in working order.
Prestwich, Manchester. *Heaton Hall.* House built in 1722 containing paintings, furniture, glass, Wedgwood pottery and English porcelain.
Rusholme, Manchester. *The Gallery of English Costume, Platt Hall.* Clothes and accessories from 17th century to the present day.
Salford. *Museum and Art Gallery.* Includes a reconstructed 19th century street and paintings by L. S. Lowry.

HAMPSHIRE (Map page 40)

Alresford. *The Mid-Hants "Watercress" Line.* Steam locomotives. Steam rides.
Andover. *Weyhill Wildlife Park.*
Beaulieu. *Maritime Museum, Buckler's Hard.* See page 31.
Beaulieu. *National Motor Museum.* See page 31.
Butser, nr Petersfield. *Butser Ancient Farm.* See page 12.
Fordingbridge. *Breamore House.* Elizabethan manor house containing furniture, tapestries and paintings. Also *Carriage Museum* and *Countryside Museum.*
Horndean, nr Portsmouth. *Queen Elizabeth Country Park Trail.* 5½km long. The park is on the A3, 2½km south of Petersfield.
Liphook. *Hollycombe Steam Collection.* Steam railways, steam swings and tramway. Woodland gardens and arboretum.
Litchfield. *Beacon Hill.* Hill fort.
Portchester. *Portchester Castle.* See page 40.
Portsmouth. *H.M.S. Victory.* See page 30.
Portsmouth. *The Portsmouth Royal Naval Museum.* Contains items connected with Nelson, ship models, figureheads and medals.
Stratfield Saye, nr Reading. *Stratfield Saye and Wellington Country Park.* Has collection illustrating the career of the first Duke of Wellington, adventure playground, model boats, animal area, nature trails. Also, the *National Dairy Museum.*
Winchester. *Marwell Zoological Park.* Wildlife in natural environments. Children's zoo and picnic area in parklands.

HEREFORD/WORCESTER (Map page 45)

Alfrick, nr Worcester. *Ravenshill Woodland Reserve Trail.* ¾km and 2½km long. Take the A44 west from Worcester, turn left after crossing River Teme at Knightsford Bridge and follow Alfrick signposts.
Bewdley. *Bewdley Museum.* Folk museum with displays of various crafts.
Bewdley. *Severn Valley Railway.* Over 30 steam locomotives. Riverside walks and picnic areas.
Bewdley. *West Midlands Safari and Leisure Park.*
Bromsgrove. *Avoncroft Museum of Buildings.* Old buildings, including a working windmill and box-framed houses.
Bromsgrove. *The Norton Collection.* Includes gramophones, wireless and crystal sets, Victorian musical boxes and kitchenware.
Eardisland, nr Leominster. *Burton Court.* Costume exhibition and model fairground.
Fladbury, nr Pershore. *Delamere Bird Garden and Aquarium.* Birds, small pets and layouts of model trains.
Hartlebury, nr Kidderminster. *Hartlebury Castle.* Contains state rooms and *Hereford and Worcester County Museum.*
Hereford. *Bulmer Railway Centre.* Displays of steam locomotives with occasional "steam" days.
Kidderminster. *Clee Hill Bird Gardens.* Over 400 birds and animals.
Kingsland, Leominster. *Croft Castle.* Dates back to the 11th century. Nearby is the Iron Age fort of *Croft Ambrey.*
Leominster. *Eye Manor.* Has displays of corn dollies, costumes, needlework, paper sculptures and costume dolls.
Malvern Wells. *Hereford Beacon.* Large hill fort.

HERTFORDSHIRE (Map pages 40–41 and 48–49)

Hatfield. *Hatfield House.* See page 18.
Hemel Hempstead. *Piccotts End Medieval Wall Paintings.* 15th century wall paintings and Elizabethan painted room, medieval well and priest's hiding hole.
Knebworth. *Knebworth House.* See page 18.
London Colney. *Salisbury Hall.* 17th century house with medieval moat. Includes *The Mosquito Aircraft Museum* with prototype of de Havilland Mosquito and other aircraft.
St Albans. *St Albans Abbey.* Begun in 11th century, it has second longest nave in England, and rare medieval wall paintings recently discovered behind old whitewash.
St Albans. *St Albans Roman (Verulamium) Museum.* See page 12.

St Albans. *Verulamium Roman Town.* See page 13.
Tring. *Tring Reservoirs Nature Trail.* 3km long. Turn off A41, between Tring and Aylesbury, on to B489. Nature Reserve car park is beyond Buckland at Startops End.
Tring. *Zoological Museum.*
Watford. *Cassiobury Park Nature Trail.* Various lengths. On A412 Watford to Rickmansworth road. Turn off at Gade Avenue and start at car park.
Welwyn. *The Roman Bath House.* Preserved in a specially constructed vault under the A1(M).

HUMBERSIDE (Map pages 50–51)

Beverley. *Skidby Mill.* Well-preserved working windmill, built in 1821.
Bridlington. *Burton Agnes Hall.* Elizabethan country house with carved ceilings, paintings, furniture and oriental china. Gardens.
Bridlington. *Sewerby Hall and Park.* Zoo and gardens, children's park and putting.
Brigg. *Elsham Hall, Country Park and Creative Centre.* Bird sanctuary, domestic animals, country trails and crafts including pottery.
Burton Constable, nr Hull. *Burton Constable.* See page 51.
Driffield. *Sledmere House.* 1787 Georgian house including furniture and paintings. Capability Brown gardens and park.
Hull. *Town Docks Museum.* Displays about fishing, whaling and shipping.
Hull. *Transport and Archaeology Museum.* Has horse-drawn vehicles and early motor cars, and local archaeology, including Roman mosaics.
Hull. *Wilberforce House and Georgian Houses.* Has collections relating to slavery, and furniture, costumes and silver.
Humberston, Cleethorpes. *Cleethorpes Leisure Park.* Walk-through aviary, dolphin pool and children's farm.
Scunthorpe. *Normanby Hall.* Furnished mansion with costumes and paintings. Nature trail, countryside centre, pottery, working blacksmith and deer park in grounds.

ISLE OF MAN (Map page 53)

Ballaugh. *Curraghs Wild Life Park.* Walk-through aviary and wader birds' aviary. Also sea lions and penguins in nature reserve.
Castletown. *Castle Rushen.* Medieval fortress.
Castletown. *Nautical Museum.* Housed in an old boathouse, includes *Peggy*, a schooner-rigged armed yacht built in 1791.
Cregneash. *Cregneash Open Air Folk Museum.* Includes a traditionally furnished crofter-fisherman's cottage, weaver's shop and smithy.
Douglas. *Douglas Horse Tramway.* Horse-drawn tramway from Victoria Pier to Manx Electric Railway Station.
Douglas. *The Manx Museum.* Manx archaeology, natural history, paintings and folk-life. Includes reconstructed 19th century farmhouse, dairy and barn.
Douglas–Laxey. *Manx Electric Railway.* Narrow gauge railway.
Douglas–Port Erin. *Isle of Man Railway.* Narrow gauge steam railway.
Laxey. *The Lady Isabella Wheel.* See page 53.
Laxey. *Snaefell Mountain Railway.* Narrow gauge railway to top of Snaefell, the island's highest mountain.
Ramsey. *"The Grove" Rural Life Museum.* An early Victorian house and outbuildings, with horse-driven threshing mill, old vehicles and agricultural equipment plus some livestock.
Snaefell Mountain. *Murrays Museum.* Veteran and vintage motorcycles, musical instruments and ancient arms.

ISLE OF WIGHT (Map page 40)

Alverstone, nr Sandown. *Riverside Walk Nature Trail.* 3km long. Off A3056, on the Apse Heath to Alverstone road. Start at the Old Mill in Alverstone.
Arreton. *Arreton Manor.* Furnished early 17th century manor house with folk museum, childhood museum and wireless museum.
Brading. *Osborn-Smith's Wax Museum.*
Brading. *The Roman Villa.* Remains of villa including mosaic pavements and hypocaust.
Brook. *Brook Nature Trail.* 2¾km long. Turn off A3055 on to Brook to Calbourne Road, and start at Seely Hall, Brook.
Chale. *Blackgang Chine.* Includes dinosaur park, maritime museum, model village, smugglers' cave, "crooked house" and hall of mirrors.
Havenstreet Station, nr Ryde. *Isle of Wight Steam Railway.* Standard gauge steam rides.
Newport. *Carisbrooke Castle Museum.* Shows history of Isle of Wight.
Seaview, nr Ryde. *Flamingo Park Bird Sanctuary.* Various kinds of birds and pets' corner.
Shorwell, nr Newport. *Yafford Mill and Farm Park.* Restored working mill. You can see waterfowl, seals and rare breeds of farm animals. Nature trail.
Yarmouth. *Fort Victoria Country Park Nature Trail.* 2km long. Take A3054 west of Yarmouth, and turn right along Westhill Lane. Start at Fort Victoria Cafe.

KENT (Map page 41)

Bekesbourne, nr Canterbury. *Howletts Zoo Park.*
Boughton Monchelsea, nr Maidstone. *Boughton Monchelsea Place.* Elizabethan manor with later alterations. Includes display of dresses, old vehicles and farm implements, Tudor kitchen and gardens. Deer park.
Chiddingstone, nr Edenbridge. *Chiddingstone Castle.* Contains furniture, pictures, Egyptian collection and Japanese swords. Lakes and caves in the grounds.
Deal. *Deal Castle.* Circular coastal fort built by Henry VIII. Has museum of local history.
Dover. *Dover Lighthouse.* See page 13.
Dover. *Roman Painted House.* Remains of a Roman town house with wall paintings and finds from Roman Dover.
Edenbridge. *Hever Castle.* 13th century moated castle with formal Italian garden.
Eynsford. *Lullingstone Villa.* Roman villa with mosaic floor.
Hythe. *Port Lympne Wildlife Zoo Park and Gardens.*
Hythe–Dungeness. *Romney, Hythe and Dymchurch Railway.* See page 30.
Maidstone. *Leeds Castle.* Furnished castle, built in the middle of a lake in landscaped parkland. Has a museum of medieval dog collars, duckery and aviary.
Maidstone. *Tyrwhitt–Drake Museum of Carriages.* Horse-drawn vehicles of all types.
Margate. *Dreamland Zoo Park.* Also, funfair.
Penshurst. *Penshurst Place.* Medieval manor house containing furniture, portraits and armour. Formal terraced gardens.
Richborough. *Richborough Castle.* Displays of Roman finds from the site.
Rochester. *Rochester Public Museum.*
Sevenoaks. *Knole.* State rooms contain rare furniture, portraits, rugs and tapestries. Deer in parklands.
Sittingbourne. *Dolphin Yard Sailing Barge Museum.* "Live" folk museum with crafts such as sailmaking and ship repairs.
Sittingbourne. *Sittingbourne and Kemsley Light Railway.* Narrow gauge steam rides.
Tenterden. *Kent and East Sussex Railway.* See page 41.

LANCASHIRE (Map page 53)

Blackburn. *Lewis Textile Museum.* Exhibition of early textile machinery.
Blackpool. *Blackpool Zoo Park.*
Blackpool. *Dr Who Exhibition.* See page 30.
Blackpool. *Louis Tussauds.* Waxwork figures of famous people.
Blackpool. *Platform 3 Model Railway.* Large model railway and railway items.
Carnforth. *Leighton Hall.* Built 1800 and contains furniture and pictures. Grounds include a collection of birds of prey.
Carnforth. *Steamtown Railway Museum.* Main line British and continental steam locomotives, model railway and collectors' corner.
Goosnargh, nr Preston. *Chingle Hall.* Moated manor house built in 1260.
Helmshore, Rossendale. *Higher Mill Museum.* Includes a waterwheel, early textile machinery, hand looms and power looms.
Lancaster. *Judges' Lodgings.* Displays of childhood in Lancashire. Also a doll collection.
Lancaster. *Lancaster Leisure Park.* Guided factory tours of Hornsea Pottery. Children's farmyard and playground, and tea garden.
Morecambe. *Marineland Oceanarium and Aquarium.*
Morecambe and Heysham. *Winged World.* Different kinds of birds and flying fruit bats.
Preston. *Harris Museum and Art Gallery.*
Preston. *Hoghton Tower.* 16th century fortified mansion. Collection of antique dolls and dolls' houses. Walled gardens and a rose garden.
Ribchester, nr Preston. *The Ribchester Museum.* Remains from the Roman site, and an excavated area showing the granaries.

LEICESTERSHIRE (Map page 48)

Belvoir, nr Grantham. *Belvoir Castle.* See page 48.
Cadeby, nr Market Bosworth. *Cadeby Light Railway, Cadeby Rectory.* Working narrow gauge railway, model railway and steam museum. Also *Cadeby Brass Rubbing Centre.*
Castle Donington. *The Donington Collection of Single-Seater Racing Cars.* See page 48.
East Midlands Airport. *Castle Donington Air Museum.* Collection of British, French and American aircraft.
Leicester. *Jewry Wall Museum and Site.* Remains of Roman and medieval town of Leicester.
Leicester. *Leicestershire Museum of Technology, Abbey Pumping Station.* Includes beam engines, steam shovel and horse-drawn vehicles. Also the history of machine knitting.
Leicester. *Newarke Houses Museum.* Local history and crafts, toys and games, clocks and mechanical musical instruments.
Loughborough. *Midlands Steam Centre.* Displays of historic steam engines, steamboat and other engines, model railway and miniature engines.
Loughborough–Rothley. *Great Central Railway.* Steam railway over 8km of track.
Lutterworth. *Stanford Hall.* House contains antiques, pictures and costumes. Garden includes a nature trail. You can also visit the *Stanford Hall Vintage Motor and Car Museum.* Rare motorcars and famous racing motorcycles.
Melton Mowbray. *Stapleford Park.* 16th century house, with tapestries, furniture, pictures and pottery figures. In the grounds are a miniature railway and "Animal Land".
Oakham. *Rutland County Museum.* Anglo-Saxon jewellery, local history, craft tool displays, farm waggons and agricultural equipment.
Oakham. *Rutland Farm Park.* Working farm including rare breeds of cattle, ponies, pigs, etc. Also a nature trail.
Sutton Cheney, nr Market Bosworth. *Battlefield of Bosworth Battle Trail.* 2½km long. On the site of the Battle of Bosworth Field 1485. The visitors' centre includes an exhibition and battle models. There is also the *Shackerstone–Market Bosworth Railway* and you can see steam engines at Shackerstone Station.
Twycross, nr Atherstone. *Twycross Zoo.* See page 30.
Woodhouse Eaves. *Broombriggs Farm and Windmill Hill Farm Trail.* 2¾km long. Off B591.

LINCOLNSHIRE (Map pages 48 and 51)

Alford. *Alford Windmill.* Six-storey, five-sail tower mill in working order. Built 1837.
Alford. *Manor House Folk Museum.* Displays include an old sweet factory, 19th century chemist's shop, craftshops, agricultural and transport galleries.
Belton, nr Grantham. *Belton House, Park and Gardens.* Includes paintings, porcelain and tapestries. The park includes woodland and lakeland trails, a miniature railway and carriage and horse museum. Also the *National Cycle Museum.*
Boston. *Boston Guildhall Museum.* You can see prison cells used in 1607 to imprison the Pilgrim Fathers. Also collections of local archaeology.
Brocklesby. *Mausoleum Woods Nature Trail.* 3km long. On A18, 1½km north of Great Limber.
Doddington, nr Lincoln. *Doddington Hall.* Elizabethan manor including furniture, pictures, textiles and porcelain. The walled gardens include a nature trail.
Gainsborough. *Gainsborough Old Hall.* 15th century manor house with medieval kitchen. Displays of furniture, dolls, period dresses and portraits. Riverside gardens.

Lincoln. *City and County Museum.* Displays about Lincoln from prehistoric to medieval times.
Lincoln. *Ellis Mill.* Four-sailed windmill in working order.
Lincoln. *Lincoln Brass Rubbing Centre, Lincoln Cathedral.*
Lincoln. *Lincoln Castle.* Built by William the Conqueror. The remains include a keep, curtain wall, gateway, three towers and a wall-walk.
Lincoln. *Lincolnshire Vintage Vehicle Society.* Cars, buses and commercial vehicles, plus old road signs, bus tickets and posters.
Lincoln. *Museum of Lincolnshire Life.*
Mablethorpe. *Mablethorpe's Animal Gardens.*
Skegness. *Church Farm Museum.* 19th century farmhouse and outbuildings housing agricultural, industrial and domestic collections.
Skegness. *Gibraltar Point Nature Reserve Nature Trail.* 3km long. South of Skegness.
Skegness. *Skegness Natureland Marine Zoo.*

LONDON (Map pages 40–41)
See pages 26–29.

MERSEYSIDE (Map page 47)

Liverpool. *Croxteth Hall and Country Park.* In the house you can see displays of costume. In the country park there is a nature trail.
Liverpool. *Liverpool Botanic Gardens.*
Liverpool. *Liverpool Docks.* Waterbus trips round the quay and boats.
Liverpool. *Merseyside County Museums.* Natural history, Merseyside land transport, horse and steam vehicles, history of shipping, African masks, etc.
Liverpool. *The Planetarium.* Daily programmes on astronomy. Also displays on the history of time-keeping and space exploration.
Liverpool. *Speke Hall.* Tudor box-framed house. Interior includes a great hall, plasterwork and furniture.
Prescot. *Knowsley Safari Park.* See page 47.
St Helens. *Pilkington Glass Museum.* History of glassmaking techniques.
Southport. *Model Village.*
Southport. *Southport Zoo.* Parrot house, aquarium and pets' corner.

NORFOLK (Map page 49)

Aylsham. *Blickling Hall.* Jacobean mansion. Parkland.
Brancaster. *Saxon Shore Fort.*
Brancaster Staithe. *Scolt Head Island.* ½km long nature trail. By boat from Brancaster Staithe harbour, on A149 between Hunstanton and Burnham Market.
Castle Rising. *Castle Rising.* Norman castle.
Cromer. *Cromer Zoo.*
Diss. *Banham International Motor Museum.* Collection of motor cars and motorcycles dating from 1920s to 1950s. Also collection of dolls and vehicle adventure playground.
Diss. *Banham Zoo.* Collection of rare primates including woolly monkeys, and other unusual animals and birds.
Diss. *Bressingham Live Steam Museum and Gardens.* Over 50 different steam engines, and narrow gauge railway rides.
East Dereham. *Bishop Bonner's Cottage.* Early 16th century cottage with rural life exhibits.
Felbrigg, nr Cromer. *Felbrigg Hall.* 17th century house with 18th century furniture and pictures. Walled garden, lakeside and woodland walks.
Great Witchingham, nr Norwich. *Norfolk Wildlife Park and Pheasant Trust.* See page 31.
Great Yarmouth. *Burgh Castle.* Remains of a Roman fort.
Great Yarmouth. *Caister Roman Town.* Remains of a Roman commercial port.
Great Yarmouth. *Maritime Museum.*
King's Lynn. *Museum of Social History.* Life in King's Lynn displayed in an 18th century house.
King's Lynn. *Sandringham House Gardens.* One of the homes of the Queen. Grounds only open, including motor car museum and nature trail.
Norwich. *Bridewell Museum of Local Industries and Rural Crafts.* Local industry from the Middle Ages to the present day, including displays of weaving, leatherwork, clockmaking, early bikes, fishing and agricultural equipment.
Norwich. *The Mustard Shop.* Colman's Mustard Museum showing how mustard is made.
Norwich. *Norwich Castle.* Contains a museum.
Norwich. *Strangers' Hall Museum of Domestic Life.* Rooms furnished in different periods from 16th to 19th century, plus costumes and textiles.
Sheringham. *North Norfolk Railway Co., Sheringham Station.* See page 49.
Sutton, nr Stalham. *Sutton Windmill.* The tallest mill in the country, with interesting machinery.
Thetford. *Kilverstone Wildlife Park.* Animals and birds of Central and South America.
Thursford, nr Fakenham. *Thursford Collection of Organs and Engines, Laurel Farm.* Includes steam road engines, mechanical musical organs and a Wurlitzer theatre organ.
Weeton. *Grimes Graves.* See page 49.
West Rudham, between King's Lynn and Fakenham. *Houghton Hall.* 18th century house built for the first Prime Minister of England, Sir Robert Walpole. You can see heavy horses and Shetland ponies in the stables.
Wroxham. *Hoveton Great Broad Nature Trail.* ¾km long. Access by boat only, from Wroxham or Horning.

NORTHAMPTONSHIRE (Map page 48)

Corby. *Rockingham Castle.* See page 48.
Daventry. *Daventry Country Park Nature Trail.* ¾km long. Take B4036 (Welton Road) from Daventry; trail starts at park entrance.
Guilsborough. *Guilsborough Grange Bird and Pet Park.*
Harlestone, nr Northampton. *Althorp.* Originally built in 1508, the house contains a good collection of pictures.
Kettering. *Boughton House.* Tudor monastic building, enlarged mainly in French style. Collections of furniture and pictures, and an armoury. Parkland, woodland and a play area.
Kettering. *Westfield Museum.* Displays of footwear, shoe-making tools and machinery.
Kettering. *Wicksteed Park.* Includes a miniature railway, adventure playground, and nature trail.
Lilford, nr Oundle. *Lilford Park.* Contains birds and animals, children's farm and adventure playground, aviaries, picnic areas.
Little Billing, Northampton. *Billing Mill.* Milling museum housed in a restored corn grinding mill. You can see the waterwheel and machinery in motion.
Naseby, nr Market Harborough. *Museum of Miniature Rural Buildings.* Miniature scale models of castles and rural buildings. Also demonstrations of thatching. You can also visit *Naseby Battle and Farm Museum* which includes a model of Naseby Battlefield, farm tools and old tractors.
Northampton. *Museum of Leathercraft.* Use of leather from Egyptian times until the present. Includes costumes, saddlery and harness.
Oundle. *Southwick Hall.* 14th century manor house, with Tudor and 18th century additions.
Stoke Bruerne, nr Northampton. *Waterways Museum.* See page 31.

NORTHUMBERLAND (Map page 52)

Alnwick. *Alnwick Castle.* See page 52.
Ashington. *Woodhorn Church.* Exhibition on history of Christianity in Northumberland.
Bamburgh. *Bamburgh Castle.*
Cambo. *Wallington Hall.* Collections of porcelain, needlework, dolls' houses and dolls.
Chillingham, nr Wooler. *Chillingham Wild White Cattle.* Herd of pure wild white cattle, which have roamed the area for 700 years. Also, *Chillingham Castle* set in a large park.
Derwent Reservoir. *Derwent Reservoir Country Trail/Countryside Motor Trail.* 20½km long. Turn west off A68 at "Manor House", and start the trail at Derwent Reservoir Dam.
Farne Islands. See page 52.
Ford. *Heatherslaw Mill.* Partially restored watermill and agricultural museum.
Glanton. *World Bird Research Station.* Wild bird sanctuary, first aid and release centre.
Hadrian's Wall. See page 13. Today, not all of the Wall is visible. Some of the important sites are:
Bardon Mill. *Chesterholm Roman Fort and Settlement.* Remains of large civilian settlement, plus full-size reconstruction of parts of the Wall and a replica of a milecastle. The museum includes finds from the site – Roman shoes and sandals, writing tablets, weapons, jewellery and textiles.
Chesters, nr Chollerford. *The Clayton Collection.* Roman weapons, tools, sculptures and other material found at Roman forts.
Corbridge. *Corbridge Roman Station.* See page 52.
Housesteads. Roman garrison remains, which include part of a Roman hospital. The museum has sculpture, pottery and inscribed stones.
Holy Island. *Lindisfarne Castle.* Built in 1550, the castle was converted into a home in 1903 and includes oak furniture and a collection of prints. Accessible at low tide by causeway.
Holy Island. *Lindisfarne Priory.* Contains Anglo-Saxon sculpture, medieval pottery and reproductions of the Lindisfarne gospels. Accessible at low tide by causeway.
Rothbury. *Cragside.* Victorian house containing much original furniture, Pre-Raphaelite pictures and experimental scientific apparatus.
Seaton Sluice. *Seaton Delaval Hall.* House, designed by Vanbrugh, containing furniture, portraits and ceramics. Gardens.
Stocksfield. *National Tractor and Farm Machinery Museum.* Over 100 tractors, and thousands of farm tools and machinery from the last 100 years.

NORTH YORKSHIRE (Map pages 50–51 and 53)

Aldborough. *The Aldborough Roman Museum.* Roman pottery, glass, coins and metalwork.
Aysgarth Falls. *The Yorkshire Museum of Carriages and Horse Drawn Vehicles.*
Boroughbridge. *The Devil's Arrows.* See page 51.
Clapham, nr Settle. *Ingleborough Cave.* Show cave with stalactites, stalagmites, etc.
Embsay, nr Skipton. *Yorkshire Dales Railway.* Small steam railway.
Grosmont–Pickering. *North York Moors Railway.* 29km of track through the National Park.
Hawes. *Upper Dales Folk Museum.* Traditional trades and occupations, including displays of hay and sheep farming, peat cutting, hand knitting, cheese making.
Helmsley. *Rievaulx Abbey.* Cistercian monastery ruins.
Hutton-le-Hole. *Ryedale Folk Museum.* Prehistoric and Roman antiquities, 19th century craft tools, domestic equipment and other displays. In the *Folk Park* are old buildings including a blacksmith's shop, Elizabethan glass furnace and a 16th century manor house.
Ingleton. *White Scar Caves.* Limestone caves with stalactites, stalagmites and waterfalls.
Kirby Misperton, nr Malton. *Flamingoland.* Zoo of over 100 animals and birds. Also jungle cruise, model railway centre and children's playground.
Kirkby Fleetham. *Wonderful World of Nature.* Exhibition of stuffed animals and natural history.
Knaresborough. *Mother Shipton's Cave, Dropping Well Estate.* See page 30.
Layerthorpe, York–Dunnington. *Derwent Valley Railway.* Standard gauge steam rides plus displays of engines.
Malham Moor, nr Settle. *Malham Tarn Nature Trail.* 2½km long. Malham Tarn Field Centre.
Malton. *Castle Howard.* See page 50.
Pateley Bridge. *Stump Cross Caverns.* Stalactites and stalagmites in floodlit caves.
Pickering. *Beck Isle Museum of Rural Life.*
Pickering. *Dalby Forest Visitor Centre, Low Dalby.* Forest walks, and displays of wildlife and local history.
Richmond. *Georgian Theatre.* Built in 1788, the country's oldest theatre still in its original form. Also, a theatre museum.
Richmond. *Richmond Castle.* See page 53.
Ripley. *Ripley Castle.* The Tudor part contains armour and the Adam part contains furniture and pictures. Gardens.
Ripon. *Fountains Abbey.* See page 50.
Ripon. *Newby Hall.* Adam house containing tapestries and sculptures. In the gardens are a miniature riverside railway, adventure garden, rock garden with waterfalls and picnic areas.
Snaith, nr Selby. *Carlton Towers.* Contains furniture, silver, china, pictures, costumes and uniforms. There is also a priest's hiding hole.
York. *Beningbrough Hall.* Built about 1716, contains 100 portraits from the National Portrait Gallery. In the Victorian laundry is an exhibition of domestic life. Gardens.
York. *The Heritage Centre.* Exhibition of the social and archaeological history of York.

York. *National Railway Museum.* See page 31.
York. *York Castle Museum.* Folk museum of Yorkshire life including period rooms, cobbled streets of shops, early crafts, toys, domestic and agricultural equipment.
York. *York Model Railway Co.* Large model railway layout.

NOTTINGHAMSHIRE (Map pages 48 and 51)

Carlton in Lindrick. *Old Mill Museum, Carlton Mill.* Mill machinery, undershot water wheel and rural tools. Also collections of butterflies, shells and country crafts.
Creswell, nr Worksop. *Creswell Crags Picnic Site and Visitor Centre.* Limestone caves and gorge. The Visitor Centre has displays of archaeological finds depicting life of Stone Age man.
Edwinstowe, nr Mansfield. *Sherwood Forest Country Park and Visitor Centre.* Audio-visual show in the Visitor Centre. See the Major Oak in the Forest, where Robin Hood and his Merry Men used to meet.
Gunthorpe, nr Lowdham. *Gunthorpe Rural Walk.* 6½km long. Start at Gunthorpe car park, opposite "Unicorn Inn".
Haughton, nr Bothamsall, Retford. *National Mining Museum, Lound Hall.* Exhibits include colliery shunting engines, coalface machinery, handtools, lamps, underground canal boat, pumping equipment, and photographs.
Linby. *Newstead Abbey.* Contains possessions of the poet Byron, including pictures and furniture. In the park are lakes, waterfalls and different types of garden.
Newark-on-Trent. *Newark Air Museum.* Displays of aircraft and aircraft parts, including engines and propellers. Also model aircraft.
Nottingham. *Museum of Costume and Textiles.* Displays include the history of lace, textiles, costumes and embroideries, dolls' clothes.
Nottingham. *Nottingham Castle.* Built in the 17th century. Now houses the *City Museum.*
Nottingham. *Nottingham Industrial Museum, Wollaton Hall.* Housed in the 18th century stables, the displays tell the stories of Nottingham's industries – printing, hosiery and lace making, and pharmacy.
Nottingham. *Wollaton Hall and Natural History Museum.* Elizabethan house, with collections of rocks, plants and animals. The gardens include a deer park and lakeside nature trail.
Worksop. *Clumber Park and Chapel.*

OXFORDSHIRE (Map pages 40 and 48)

Banbury. *Broughton Castle.* Built in 1300, with Tudor additions. Contents include furniture and arms and armour.
Burford. *Cotswold Wildlife Park.* Walk-through aviary, plus animals, including red pandas, in their natural surroundings. Also narrow gauge railway and adventure playground.
Burford. *Tolsey Museum.* Illustrates the effect of England's history on a small country town.
Cogges, nr Witney. *Manor Farm Museum.* Edwardian farm, including kitchens, dairy and animals. Also nature trail and historic trail.
Combe, nr Woodstock. *Combe Mill.* Built in 1852, includes a working beam engine. You can also see a blacksmith at work.
Didcot. *Didcot Railway Centre.* Great Western Railway steam engines in original engine shed. Steam train rides.
Henley-on-Thames. *Greys Court.* 16th century house with 18th century furniture and miniature rooms, some showing scenes from the past, farm interiors, etc. Gardens.
Henley-on-Thames. *Stonor Park.* Built over many centuries, includes furniture, portraits, stained glass and Italian sculpture. Wooded deer park.
Oxford. *The Ashmolean Museum of Art and Archaeology.* Collections include archaeology, paintings, ceramics, sculpture and silver.
Oxford. *Museum of the History of Science.* Includes early scientific instruments such as astrolabes, microscopes, medical and photographic equipment. Also clocks.
Oxford. *University Botanic Gardens.*
Mapledurham, nr Reading (Berks.). *Mapledurham House.* See page 40.
Steeple Aston. *Rousham House.* 17th century house containing furniture and portraits. In the gardens are waterfalls and statues.
Witney. *North Leigh.* Remains of a Roman building laid out round a courtyard, including a mosaic pavement.
Woodstock. *Blenheim Palace.* See page 18. You can see pictures, tapestries and a Churchill exhibition. There are gardens, boat trips on the lake and a narrow gauge steam railway.

SCILLY ISLES (Map page 42)

St Mary's. *Porth Hellick Down.* Group of five tombs, either Stone Age or Bronze Age.
St Mary's. *St Mary's Museum.* Natural history, archaeology and geology of the Isles, plus treasure from ancient shipwrecks.
Tresco. *Cromwell's Castle.* Round tower dating from the 17th century.
Tresco. *Tresco Abbey.* Sub-tropical gardens including palms and yuccas.
Tresco. *Valhalla Maritime Museum.* Includes figureheads and ships' ornaments salvaged from ships wrecked in the area.

SHROPSHIRE (Map pages 45 and 47)

Acton Scott, nr Church Stretton. *Acton Scott Working Farm Museum.* Working farm using heavy horses, demonstrating 19th century farming techniques and traditional crafts. You can see various old breeds of animals.
Aston Munslow, nr Craven Arms. *The White House Museum of Buildings and Country Life.* Buildings of various periods on the site of a Saxon township. Interiors include tools, utensils, etc., used in domestic life and farming.
Bridgnorth. *Midland Motor Museum.* More than 55 vehicles, including sports cars and motor cycles. Also bird garden and lake.
Bridgnorth. *Severn Valley Railway.* 20km steam ride alongside River Trent to Bewdley.
Burwarton, Cleobury North. *Brown Clee Nature Trail.* 2km long. B4364 to Cleobury North. Burwarton is about 1½km west of Cleobury North.
Craven Arms. *Stokesay Castle.* See page 45.
Hilton, nr Bridgnorth. *Hilton Valley Railway.* Miniature steam locomotive trips.
Hopton Bank, Cleobury Mortimer. *Clee Hill Bird and Animal Gardens.*
Ironbridge, Telford. *Ironbridge Gorge Museum.* See page 31.
Ludlow. *Ludlow Castle.*
Old Coleham, Shrewsbury. *Coleham Pumping Station.* Preserved beam engines.
Oswestry. *Tyn-y-Rhos Hall.* Fully furnished in late 19th century style, including carved oak stairway and fireplace.
Shifnal. *Weston Park.* See page 47.
Wroxeter. *Wroxeter Roman City.* Remains include a Roman bath house, and the finds are in the *Viroconium Museum.*

SOMERSET (Map page 43)

Cheddar. *Cheddar Caves Museum and Exhibition.* The caves contain coloured stalactites and stalagmites. In Gough's Cave you can see the skeleton of a Stone Age man, plus tools, flints and weapons. In the *Cheddar Motor Museum* are veteran cars and bicycles.
Cloutsham, Porlock. *Cloutsham Nature Trail.* 5km long. On B3224, west of Wheddon Cross on A396.
Cranmore, nr Shepton Mallet. *East Somerset Railway, Cranmore Station.* Standard gauge steam railway. There are 8 steam engines.
Cricket St Thomas, nr Chard. *The West Country Wildlife Park.* Woodland and lakes with wild animals, including zebra and llamas, and birds.
Glastonbury. *Glastonbury Abbey.*
Glastonbury. *Somerset Rural Life Museum.* Horse-drawn agricultural machinery and vehicles, farmhouse kitchen, cider making, withy cutting and Cheddar cheese displays.
Minehead–Bishop's Lydeard. *West Somerset Railway.* 32km of track. Diesel rides all year round, steam rides in the summer.
Montacute. *Montacute House.* See page 43.
Street. *Street Shoe Museum.* Shoes from Roman times until now, shoe machinery 1860–1920.
Washford Station, nr Watchet. *Somerset and Dorset Railway.* Short steam rides.
Wookey Hole. *Wookey Hole Caves.* See page 43.
Yeovilton. *Fleet Air Arm Museum.* See page 43.

SOUTH YORKSHIRE (Map page 51)

Cawthorne. *Cannon Hall.* Contains 18th century furniture, paintings and glassware. Parkland.
Rotherham. *Clifton Park Museum.* 18th century furnished rooms and period kitchen. Also displays of Victoriana, glass and glassmaking equipment, local natural history, etc.
Rotherham. *Conisbrough Castle.* See page 51.
Sheffield. *Abbeydale Industrial Hamlet.* See page 47.
Sheffield. *Rivelin Nature Trail.* 3km long. Rails Road, Western Sheffield. Take the A57 or A6101.
Sheffield. *Sheffield City Museum.*
Worsbrough, nr Barnsley. *Worsbrough Mill Museum.* Country park setting for a working industrial museum.

STAFFORDSHIRE (Map page 47)

Alton, nr Cheadle. *Alton Towers.* Gardens include tower ruins, aerial cable cars, miniature railway, aquarium, pony and donkey rides and woodland walks.
Barlaston, Stoke-on-Trent. *Josiah Wedgwood & Sons Ltd.* Visitor Centre includes a craft demonstration area, museum and galleries.
Brownhills. *Chasewater Light Railway, Chasewater Pleasure Park.* Locomotives and rolling stock dating from 1875 to1975. Other railway relics.
Burton-on-Trent. *Bass Museum of Brewing.* See page 48.
Cheddleton, nr Leek. *Cheddleton Flint Mill.* Two preserved watermills, used for grinding flint for the pottery industry.
Cheddleton, nr Leek. *Cheddleton Railway Museum.* Two steam locomotives, coaches, etc.
Codsall, nr Wolverhampton. *Codsall Nature Trail.* 4km long. Take A41 from Wolverhampton, turn right after "Crown" at Wergs. Trail starts in Oaken Lanes just before Codsall.
Dilhorne, nr Cheadle. *Foxfield Light Railway Society Ltd.* Steam train from Foxfield to Blythe Bridge – 11km there and back.
Fenton, Stoke-on-Trent. *Crown Staffordshire, Minerva Works.* 1½ hour tour, from making to final firing of chinaware and florals.
Hanley, Stoke-on-Trent. *Spitfire Museum.*
Hoar Cross, nr Burton-on-Trent. *Hoar Cross Hall.* Includes European armour, Victorian furnishings, pictures and costumes.
Lichfield. *Hanch Hall.* Built in the 13th century, with later additions. Collections of teapots, dolls, shells, needlework and costumes.
Longton, Stoke-on-Trent. *Gladstone Pottery Museum.* See page 31.
Shugborough, Stafford. *Staffordshire County Museum and Mansion House.* House has 18th century furniture, pictures and silver. The museum has a brewhouse, coachhouse and laundry. At *Shugborough Park Farm* you can see cattle, pigs, sheep and agricultural equipment.
Tamworth. *Drayton Manor Park and Zoo.*
Tamworth. *Tamworth Castle and Museum.* 12th century keep and tower, with later additions. Includes furniture and woodwork.
Tunstall, Stoke-on-Trent. *Chatterley Whitfield Mining Museum.* Underground coal workings and engine houses, winding equipment, etc., illustrating mining life at the turn of the century.
Wall, nr Lichfield. *Wall Roman Site.* Remains of Letocetum posting station and baths. Finds from the excavation are displayed in museum.

SUFFOLK (Map page 49)

Bury St Edmunds. *The Gersholm–Parkington Memorial Collection of Clocks and Watches.*
Bury St Edmunds. *Ickworth.* Built 1794–1830. Contains furniture, silver and pictures. Orangery and woodland walk in gardens.
Earsham, nr Bungay. *Otter Trust.* See page 31.
Framlingham. *Framlingham Castle.* See page 15.
Helmingham, nr Debenham. *Helmingham Hall Gardens.* Moated Elizabethan gardens, including Highland cattle and a safari ride in the deer park.
Ipswich. *Christchurch.* Tudor house with furniture from Tudor to Victorian times. Garden.
Ipswich. *Ipswich Museum and Art Gallery.* Includes replicas of the Sutton Hoo Saxon treasure hoard and the Mildenhall Roman silver treasure.
Kessingland, nr Lowestoft. *Suffolk Wildlife and Country Park.*

Lavenham. *Guildhall.* Box-framed 16th century building containing old furniture and tools.
Lowestoft. *East Anglia Transport Museum.* Includes trams, trolleybuses, cars and buses.
Lowestoft. *Maritime Museum.* Models of boats, plus shipwrights tools, etc.
Lowestoft. *Somerleyton Hall.* State rooms include paintings and carvings. In the gardens are a maze, garden trail and miniature railway.
Orford. *Orford Castle.* Has an 18-sided keep.
Saxtead Green, nr Framlingham. *Saxtead Green Windmill.* 18th century 3-storey post mill restored to perfect condition.
Stonham Aspall, nr Ipswich. *Jigsaw Puzzle Centre.* Showrooms and workshops. Jigsaws are hand cut from wood and silk-screen printed.
Sudbury. *Gainsborough's House.* Gainsborough's birthplace including some of his possessions, and paintings by him and Constable.
Wickham Market. *Easton Farm Park.* See page 31.
West Stow, nr Bury St Edmunds. *West Stow Anglo-Saxon Village.* Four buildings constructed by Anglo-Saxon methods and materials. Forest trail. Good for walks and picnics.
Woodbridge. *Woodbridge Tide Mill.* Present watermill built about 1800 and been restored.

SURREY (Map pages 40–41)

Brockham Pits, nr Dorking. *Brockham Museum Trust.* (Unmarked farm track on north side of A25 Dorking–Reigate road.) Narrow gauge steam and diesel engines.
Charlwood. *Gatwick Garden Aviaries and Children's Zoo.*
Chertsey, nr Staines. *Thorpe Park.* See page 30.
Chessington. *Chessington Zoo.* Includes penguin pool and hippo wallow, models of dinosaurs, Punch and Judy and a miniature railway.
Dorking. *Polesden Lacey.* Collections of furniture, tapestries and pictures. The garden includes topiary and rose garden.
Esher. *Claremont Landscape Garden.* Includes a lake and a grotto.
Farnham. *Old Kiln Agricultural Museum.* Farm implements, waggons and hand tools. Also an old kitchen, forge and wheelwright's shop.
Godalming. *Winkworth Arboretum.* Wide variety of trees and shrubs and two lakes.
Guildford. *Loseley House.* Elizabethan mansion including panelling, fine ceilings, furniture, tapestries and needlework.
Haslemere. *Haslemere Educational Museum.* Displays of British birds, zoology, botany, geology and local industries.
Headley, nr Leatherhead. *Nower Wood Nature Trails.* 1½km and 2¾km long. Start at car park on B2033, about 5km from Leatherhead.
Hold Pond, nr Farnham. *Birdworld Zoological Gardens.* Tropical bird collection.
West Clandon, nr Guildford. *Clandon Park.* 18th century Classical style house including furniture, porcelain and an old kitchen.
Wisley, Ripley. *Wisley Garden.*

TYNE & WEAR (Map page 50)

Newcastle. *Bagpipe Museum.*
Newcastle. *Hancock Museum.* Natural history displays including plant and animal fossils, and British mammals.
Newcastle. *Museum of Antiquities.* Prehistoric, Roman and Anglo-Saxon material.
Newcastle. *Science Museum.* Exhibits ranging from shipbuilding, engineering and transport to mining and electricity.
Newcastle. *Stanley Zoo.* On the banks of an old mill stream, includes a tropical house, reptile house and aquarium.
St Mary's Island, Whitley Bay. *St Mary's Island Nature Trail.* 2km long. On A193, north of Whitley Bay. Watch out for the lighthouse and sign posts, and start at car park by Curry's Point.
South Shields. *Arbeia Roman Fort Museum.* Objects found at the site of the Roman Fort.
Springwell, nr Gateshead. *Bowes Railway.* Standard gauge steam engines.
Sunderland. *Monkwearmouth Station Museum.* 1848 station with restored original booking office. Exhibits trace history of local land transport.
Sunderland. *Ryhope Engines Museum.* Water pumping station with two 1868 beam engines, which are run under steam power.

Washington. *Washington Old Hall.* Jacobean manor house. Ancestral home of George Washington, first President of the U.S.A. Furnished.
Washington. *Washington Wildfowl Refuge.* See page 50.

WARWICKSHIRE (Map page 48)

Alcester. *Ragley Hall.* See page 48.
Dorsington, nr Stratford-upon-Avon. *The Domestic Fowl Trust, Dorsington Manor.* Rare breeds of ducks, geese, turkeys, etc.
Henley in Arden. *Henley Bird Gardens.*
Kenilworth. *Kenilworth Castle.* Built in 1120.
Kenilworth. *Stoneleigh Abbey.* Abbey and park, gardens and woodlands.
Nuneaton. *Arbury Hall.* Elizabethan and 18th century Gothic house and gardens. Displays of motorcycles, veteran cycles and farm implements in the stables.
Shottery, nr Stratford-upon-Avon. *Anne Hathaway's Cottage.*
Southam, nr Leamington Spa. *Southam Zoo Farm.*
Stratford-upon-Avon. *Hall's Croft.* Furnished Tudor house with walled garden.
Stratford-upon-Avon. *Louis Tussaud's Waxworks.* Waxwork figures of famous actors in scenes from Shakespeare's plays.
Stratford-upon-Avon. *Royal Shakespeare Theatre Picture Gallery and Museum.*
Stratford-upon-Avon. *Shakespeare's Birthplace.* Box-framed house with Shakespeare exhibits.
Stratford-upon-Avon. *Stratford-upon-Avon Motor Museum.* Vintage cars including Rolls-Royce and Mercedes-Benz. Also sports and racing cars, and motorcycles. Picnic garden.
Tysoe. *Compton Wynyates.* See page 48.
Warwick. *Warwick Castle.* 14th century castle including dungeons, torture chamber, ghost tower and armoury. Peacock gardens.
Warwick. *Warwick Doll Museum, Oken's House.*
Warwick. *The National Philatelic Centre.*
Wilmcote, nr Stratford-upon-Avon. *Mary Arden's House.* Tudor farmhouse with farm museum.

WEST MIDLANDS (Map pages 45 and 48)

Bagington, nr Coventry. *Lunt Roman Fort.* See page 13.
Bagington, nr Coventry. *Midland Air Museum.* Civil and military aircraft, plus the aircraft used in the film "Battle of Britain".
Birmingham. *Birmingham Botanical Centre.* Gardens with greenhouses of tropical and other plants. Tropical and other birds, pets' corner and play area.
Birmingham. *Birmingham Museum of Science and Industry.* Engineering, locomotive, transport and aircraft displays, including several press-button exhibits.
Birmingham. *Birmingham Nature Centre.* British and European mammals, birds and reptiles.
Birmingham. *Birmingham Railway Museum.* Collection of standard gauge steam engines.
Birmingham. *Sarehole Mill.* 18th century water-powered corn mill. One wheel is working, and there is a display of milling items.
Coventry. *Coombe Abbey Bird Garden.*
Coventry. *Coventry Brass Rubbing Centre, Coventry Cathedral.*
Coventry. *Coventry Toy Museum.* 6,000 toys dating back to 1760, including dolls, trains, games and amusement machines.
Coventry. *Coventry Zoo Park.*
Dudley. *Black Country Museum.* Rebuilt buildings on a restored canal, reconstructing the past of the Midlands.
Dudley. *Dudley Zoo.* See page 45.
West Bromwich. *Oak House.* Tudor house with panelled rooms and 16th and 17th century oak furniture.

WEST SUSSEX (Map pages 40–41)

Arundel. *Arundel Castle.* Built in Norman times, restored in 18th and 19th centuries. Includes armour, furniture and paintings.
Arundel. *Arundel Wildfowl Reserve.* Includes black swans and tree-nesting ducks.
Arundel. *Potter's Museum of Curiosity.* Stuffed animals displayed in natural settings.
Bignor. *Bignor Roman Villa.* Remains include mosaics, jewellery, pottery and a hypocaust.

Bognor Regis. *Zootopia.* Large collection of animals.
Bramber. *St Mary's.* 15th century box-framed house, including handicrafts and furniture.
Chichester. *Weald and Downland Open Air Museum.* See page 31.
Fishbourne, Chichester. *The Roman Palace.* See pages 13 and 40.
Goodwood. *Goodwood House.* Contains furniture, tapestries, porcelain and pictures.
Henfield. *Woods Mill Nature Trail.* 1km long. On A2037, start at the watermill.
Horsham. *Horsham Museum.* In 16th century box-framed house. Displays of costumes, jewellery, toys, early bicycles, local history, etc.
Petworth. *Petworth House.* Fine collection of paintings, including some by Turner, who painted here. Gardens by Capability Brown.
Pulborough. *Parham.* Elizabethan house including a long gallery. Contains furniture, armour, tapestries and needlework. Deer park.
Sharpthorne, nr Forest Row (E. Sussex). *Tanyard.* Medieval tannery with later additions. Has open fireplaces, oak beams and furniture. Walled garden.
South Harting, nr Petersfield. *Uppark.* 1690 house with 18th century furnishings, Victorian kitchen and Queen Anne dolls' house. Gardens.
Warnham. *The Warnham War Museum.* World War II vehicles and uniforms, and relics of the Battle of Britain.
West Stoke, Chichester. *Kingley Vale National Nature Reserve Nature Trail.* 3km long. West Stoke is 5½km north east of Chichester. Car park near church, then walk north on footpath for 1km to southern edge of the Reserve.

WEST YORKSHIRE (Map pages 47, 51 and 53)

Aberford, nr Leeds. *Lotherton Hall.* Edwardian house. Contains pictures, silver, furniture, porcelain and costumes. Gardens.
Batley. *Yorkshire Fire Museum.* See page 31.
Bradford. *Bolling Hall.* Manor house with rooms furnished in styles from 16th to 19th centuries.
Bradford. *Industrial Museum.* Includes mill manager's house, 4-storey mill with woollen and worsted industry collection, plus displays of other local industries.
Halifax. *West Yorkshire Folk Museum, Shibden Hall.* 1420 box-framed house containing 17th century furniture. Also displays of coaches, harness, early agricultural equipment and craft workshops. Park.
Haworth. *Brontë Parsonage Museum.* See page 53.
Hebden Bridge. *Heptonstall Old Grammar School Museum.* Contains 17th century school furniture and local farm and domestic items.
Ilkley. *Ilkley Moor Nature Trail and Ilkley Moor Geology Trail.* 2½km to 3km. Start at the Paddling Pool, Ilkley.
Keighley. *Cliffe Castle Discovery Trail.* Various lengths. Leave Keighley on the A629, turn left up Springs Gardens Lane, and Cliffe Castle Car Park is on the right.
Keighley–Oxenhope. *Worth Valley Railway.* Standard gauge steam train rides.
Kirkstall. *Kirkstall Abbey Museum.* See page 51.
Leeds. *Harewood House and Bird Garden.* See pages 18 and 51.
Leeds–Middleton Park. *Middleton Railway.* Standard gauge steam and diesel engines. Steam rides.
Ripponden. *Pennine Farm Museum.* Typical small farm of 1800–1850. Includes kitchen, dairy, loom chamber and agricultural equipment.
Tong, nr Bradford. *Tong Cockersdale Countryside Trail No. 3.* 8km long. Start at Tong Hall in Tong, south east of Bradford.
Wakefield. *Nostell Priory.* 18th century house containing furniture and pictures. Also contains *Aircraft Museum* and *Vintage and Veteran Motorcycle Museum.*
Wetherby. *Bramham Park.* Queen Anne mansion with furniture, pictures and porcelain. Landscaped grounds.

WILTSHIRE (Map pages 40 and 43)

Amesbury. *Stonehenge.* See page 12.
Avebury. *Avebury Henge.* See page 45.
Avebury. *Wiltshire Rural Life Museum.*
Beckhampton. *Silbury Hill.* Prehistoric man-made mound 40m high, the largest in Europe.

Brokerswood, nr Westbury. *The Woodland Park Trails.* Various walks up to 1½km long. Leave A36 at Standerwick, and go through Rudge to reach Brokerswood.
Calne. *Bowood.* Exhibition rooms include costumes, furniture, sculpture and water colours. Garden includes a lake and arboretum.
Hungerford. *Littlecote.* Tudor manor including great hall, chapel and haunted bedroom.
Lacock, nr Chippenham. *Fox Talbot Museum.* Photography museum.
Lacock, nr Chippenham. *Lacock Abbey.* 13th century abbey converted into a house in 1540, with 18th century Gothic additions.
Marlborough. *Avebury Manor.* Elizabethan manor house including plasterwork, panelling and furniture.
Salisbury. *Old Sarum.* Earliest remains are Iron Age, but most of the visible parts are Norman.
Salisbury. *Salisbury and South Wiltshire Museum.*
Salisbury. *Wilton House.* Includes furniture, paintings, and display of 7,000 model soldiers set in diorama scenes. Gardens.
Swindon. *Great Western Railway Museum.* Great Western Railway engines models, nameplates, posters, tickets, etc.
Warminster. *The Lions of Longleat, Longleat Park.* See page 30.
Warminster. *Longleat House.* See page 18.
West Kennet. *West Kennet Long Barrow.* Well-preserved Stone Age burial chamber and entrance passage.
Wroughton, nr Swindon. *Barbury Castle.* Iron Age hill fort.

WALES

CLWYD (Map pages 46–47)

Abergele. *Gwrych Castle.* Jousting tournaments.
Bwlchgwyn, nr Wrexham. *The Geological Museum of North Wales.* Dinosaur display, "Time Tunnel" showing geological development of North Wales over 600 million years, geology trail in quarry and "stone" garden.
Chirk, nr Llangollen. *Chirk Castle.* Built 1310 by Edward I. Contains portraits, armour and a 4-poster bed. Gardens.
Colwyn Bay. *Dinosaur World.* "Watch and hear" the dinosaurs in the park.
Colwyn Bay. *The Welsh Mountain Zoo and Botanic Gardens.*
Llangollen. *The Canal Exhibition Centre.* Tells story of canals using working and static models, pictures, slides and other exhibits.
Llangollen. *Plas Newydd Museum.* Housed in 18th century box-framed mansion.
Rhos-on-Sea, Colwyn Bay. *Harlequin Puppet Theatre.* On the promenade.
Rhuddlan. *Bodrhyddan Hall.* Late 17th century manor. Contains armour, furniture and paintings.
Rhyl. *Dolphinarium.*
St Asaph, nr Rhyl. *St Asaph Cathedral.* Said to be the smallest cathedral in Britain. Founded AD537, but much altered in 1800s. Museum.
Wrexham. *Dolls' House.* Museum of dolls and antique dolls' house furniture.
Wrexham. *Erddig Hall.* See page 47.

DYFED (Map page 44)

Aberaeron. *Aberaeron Aquarium.*
Aberystwyth. *Aberystwyth Cliff Railway.* Cable cars go up to the top of Constitution Hill.
Aberystwyth. *Brynn-Eithyn Hall Folk Museum.* Welsh furniture, handcarts, model sailing ships, arms and armour.
Aberystwyth–Devil's Bridge. *Vale of Rheidol Railway.* See page 44.
Bronwydd Arms Station, nr Carmarthen. *Gwili Railway.* Standard gauge steam train rides.
Llandysul. *Maesllyn Woollen Mill Museum.* Working mill museum with weaving demonstrations. Nature trails in grounds.
Llandysul. *Museum of the Welsh Woollen Industry.* History and machinery of the woollen industry from the Middle Ages onwards.
Newport. *Pentre Ifan Cromlech.* See page 44.
Pendine, nr Carmarthen. *Pendine Wildlife Park.* Animals, birds, miniature railway and pottery.
Plwmp. *West Wales Farm Park.* Rare breeds of animals, children's corner and adventure playground.
Ponterwyd, nr Aberystwyth. *Llywernog Silver-Lead Mine.* Restored water-powered silver-lead mine with a flood-lit underground tunnel.
St Catherine's Island. *St Catherine's Island Zoo.* In an island fortress, accessible by foot only, when the tide is out.
Tenby. *Manor House Leisure Park.* Aquarium, pets' corner and model railway.
Trevine. *Carreg Samson Cromlech.* Stone Age burial chamber.

GWENT (Map page 45)

Abercarn, nr Newport. *Cwmcarn Scenic Forest Drive.* 11km drive through forest, which has adventure play areas, picnic areas and walks.
Abergavenny. *Abergavenny and District Museum, The Castle.* Includes a kitchen, displays on rural crafts and dresses.
Caerleon. *Roman Amphitheatre.* See page 13. Also the *Legionary Museum,* which has displays of finds from the Roman site.
Caerwent. *Caerwent Roman Site and Walls.* You can see the gateways, and the remains of houses and a forge from the old Roman town.
Caldicot. *Caldicot Castle Museum.* Displays of local history, furniture and costumes.
Llandegfedd, nr Usk. *Llandegfedd Farm Park.* Over 30 breeds of animals, some rare. Pets' corner.
Llangwm, nr Chepstow. *Wolvernewton Folk Museum.* Domestic and agricultural items.
Newport. *Tredegar Park House.* 17th century house. In the grounds are a children's farm, aquarium and boating lake.
Raglan. *Raglan Castle.* 14th–15th century moated castle.
Tintern. *Angiddy Valley.* You can see old mills and a tin plate works. Picnic areas.
Whitson, nr Newport. *Whitson Zoo.*

GWYNEDD (Map page 46)

Bangor. *Bangor Art Gallery and Museum of Welsh Antiquities.* Collections illustrate the history of North Wales.
Bangor. *Penrhyn Castle.* Built in 19th century. Has a collection of 1,000 dolls, plus stuffed birds and animals, insects and a locomotive museum.
Blaenau Ffestiniog. *Gloddfa Ganol Mountain Centre.* See page 46.
Blaenau Ffestiniog. *Llechwedd Slate Caverns.* Tramway rides through the mine workings, and demonstrations by quarrymen.
Caernarfon. *Segontium Roman Fort Museum.* On the site of an old Roman fort, and houses finds excavated there.
Conwy. *Conwy Castle.* See page 46.
Dolgellau. *Talywaen Farm Trail.* Take Cader Road from Dolgellau, and turn right at Talywaen sign 1½km on.
Fairbourne–Barmouth Ferry. *Fairbourne Railway.* Smallest little railway – only 38cm wide. 3km journey.
Great Ormes Head. *Great Orme Nature Trail.* 8km trail, but you can break off earlier and return by tram or cablecar.
Holyhead Island. *South Stack Nature Trail.* Guided walk to lighthouse.
Isle of Anglesey. *Beaumaris Gaol.* Old Victorian gaol.
Llanbedr. *Cefn Isa Farm Trail.* 2½km long. Turn inland off A496 at Llanbedr, follow signs to Cwm Bychan and Cwm Nantcol. Trail is 90m beyond Salem chapel.
Llanbedr. *Maes Artro Craft Village.* Craft demonstrations, including weaving and pottery. Also a recreated 18th century Welsh street. Adventure playground and aquarium.
Llanberis. *Llanberis Lake Railway.* 3km trip along Llyn Padarn to Penilyn, and back. Nature trail.
Llanberis. *North Wales Quarrying Museum.* Machinery and equipment depicting the local slate quarrying industry.
Llanberis–Snowdon Summit. *Snowdon Mountain Railway.* 60 minute journey by rack-and-pinion railway.
Llandudno. *Doll Museum and Model Railway.* See page 31.
Llanfairpwll, Isle of Anglesey. *Plas Newydd.* 18th century house by Menai Strait. Has a military museum. Garden.
Llanrwst. *Encounter – North Wales Museum of Wildlife.* Collections of big game trophies, wildlife of Snowdonia and rare birds.
Llanuwchllyn–Bala. *Bala Lake Railway.* Runs along Bala Lake, the largest in Wales.
Menai Bridge. *Museum of Childhood.* See page 46.
Porthmadog–Tanygrisiau. *Ffestiniog Railway.* Plus, *Ffestiniog Railway Museum.*
Portmeirion. Private village, where each house is built in a different Italian architectural style. Also *Gwyllt Gardens* which include woodland walks.
Tywyn. *The Narrow Gauge Railway Museum.* Includes British and foreign locomotives, some over 100 years old.
Tywyn–Nant Gwernol. *Talyllyn Railway.*

MID GLAMORGAN (Map pages 44–45)

Aberdare. *Dare Valley.* Moorland including ponds and waterfalls. You can follow an Industrial Trail, telling the development of coal-mining in the area. Playground and picnic areas.
Caerphilly. *Caerphilly Castle.* See page 44.
Porthcawl. *Coney Beach Amusement Park and Pleasure Beach.* Model village, dinosaur park, rides, games and sideshows.

POWYS (Map pages 44–45 and 46–47)

Abercrave. *Dan-yr-Ogof Caves.* See page 44.
Brecon. *Brecon Castle.* Remains of an 11th century castle. 3km away is a partly restored Roman fort.
Crickhowell. *Tretower Court and Castle.* Stone and timber medieval home.
Llandrindod Wells. *Castell Collen.* Well-preserved Roman fort.
Llandrindod Wells. *Llandrindod Wells Museum.* Doll collection, and history of Llandrindod Wells.
Llandrindod Wells. *Tom Norton's Collection of Old Cycles and Tricycles.*
Llanfair Caereinion–Sylfaen. *Welshpool and Llanfair Railway.* 9km journey through open countryside.
Llanidloes. *Hafren Cascades.* Forest area including waterfalls and nature trails.
Machynlleth. *Centre for Alternative Technology.* A working demonstration, set in an old slate quarry, of the use of solar, water and wind-powered machinery, etc.
Newtown. *Textile Museum.* Housed in an old handloom weaving factory, the collections include machinery, handlooms and costumes.
Welshpool. *Powis Castle.*
Welshpool. *Powysland Museum.* Folk-life of area and archaeological material including replicas of a local Roman hoard.

SOUTH GLAMORGAN (Map pages 44–45)

Barry, *Porthkerry Park.* Beach and wooded valley containing woodland trail, picnic areas, etc.
Cardiff. *Castell Coch.* 13th century foundations with Victorian reconstruction in Gothic style. Ornate painted rooms.
Cardiff. *The National Museum of Wales.* Story of Wales in six departments – plants, rocks, animals, archaeology, art and industry. Holiday activities for children.
Cardiff. *Welsh Folk Museum, St Fagans Castle.* See page 45.
Cardiff. *Welsh Industrial and Maritime Museum.*
Tinkinswood. *Stone Age Burial Chamber.*

WEST GLAMORGAN (Map page 44)

Aberavon, nr Port Talbot. *Aberavon Promenade and Afan Lido.* Includes a funfair, sports hall, boating, swimming and paddling pools.
Afan Argoed, nr Port Talbot. *Afan Argoed Country Park.* Includes five nature walks and a picnic area. Also *The Welsh Miners Museum* with displays of the history and development of the coal mining industry in South Wales, including replicas of the coal face and a miner's cottage.
Cilfrew, nr Neath. *Penscynor Wildlife Park.* See page 44.
Knelston. *Gower Farm Trail.* 9½km long plus shorter walks. Llandewi Castle Farm, just west of Knelston on A4118.
Port Talbot. *Margam Park.* Includes 100m long orangery. In the gardens are signposted walks, adventure playground and picnic areas.
Rhosili. *Gower Coast Nature Trail.* 5km long. Take A4118, west of Swansea, turn off on to the B4247 and start at car park in Rhosili.
Swansea. *Maritime and Industrial Museum.*

SCOTLAND

BORDERS (Map page 52)

Dryburgh, nr Melrose. *Dryburgh Abbey.* Ruins of 12th century abbey.
Hawick. *Hawick Museum and Art Gallery.* Geology, natural history, local history, coins and medals. In *Wilton Lodge Park,* which has gardens and riverside walks.
Hermitage, nr Newcastleton. *Hermitage Castle.* 13th century castle connected with Mary Queen of Scots. It has 4 towers and a curtain wall.
Innerleithen. *Traquair House.* Mansion dating from 10th century, containing embroideries, glass, pictures, books, an 18th century library and a secret staircase. There is a working 18th century brewhouse, craft workshops and woodland walks.
Jedburgh. *Castle Jail Museum.* Reconstructed rooms from early 19th century prison.
Jedburgh. *Jedburgh Abbey.* See page 52.
Jedburgh. *Mary Queen of Scots' House.* Museum containing relics associated with Mary Queen of Scots.
Kelso. *Floors Castle.* 18th century Adam mansion containing tapestries, furniture, paintings and porcelain. Gardens.
Kelso. *Kelso Abbey.* Ruins of 12th century abbey.
Mellerstain, nr Kelso. *Mellerstain House.* Furnished 18th century Adam mansion. Italian gardens and lake in grounds.
Melrose. *Abbotsford House.* Home of novelist Sir Walter Scott, with his collection of historic relics, armouries and huge library.
Melrose. *Melrose Abbey.* Ruins of 12th century abbey.
Peebles. *Neidpath Castle.* 14th century castle built on hill by River Tweed. Good views.
Selkirk. *Bowhill.* 19th century house with paintings, furniture and a restored Victorian kitchen. Adventure woodland and nature trails.
Selkirk. *Halliwell's House.* Ironmongery museum.
Smailholm, nr Kelso. *Smailholm Tower.* 17m high peel tower built in 16th century to guard Scottish/English border.
Walkerburn, nr Innerleithen. *Scottish Museum of Wool Textiles.*

CENTRAL (Map pages 54 and 57)

Blair Drummond, nr Doune. *Blair Drummond African Safari Park.* See page 54.
Bo'ness. *Bo'ness Museum.* Local industrial history, with pottery, cast-iron work and items connected with James Watt.
Dollar, nr Alloa. *Castle Campbell.* 15th century castle on a hill. Good views and woodland walks.
Doune. *Doune Castle.* Ruined medieval castle.
Doune. *Doune Motor Museum.* Vintage and post-vintage cars.
Falkirk. *Scottish Railway Preservation Society.* See page 57.
Grangemouth. *"Paraffin" Young Trail.* Car trail tracing the life of James "Paraffin" Young and the development of the oil industry, which he founded. Start from BP Information Centre.
Loch Katrine. *S.S. Sir Walter Scott.* Trips on this old steamer start from east end of loch.
Loch Venacher. *Invertrossachs Nature Reserve.* On south side of loch. Nature trail.
Stirling. *Bannockburn.* Exhibition at visitor centre tells you story of battle of Bannockburn, where the Scots defeated the English in 1314.
Stirling. *Landmark Visitor Centre.* Films and slides tell story of Stirling castle and town.
Stirling. *Stirling Castle.* See page 54.

DUMFRIES AND GALLOWAY (Maps pages 52 and 55)

Castle Douglas. *Threave Castle.* See page 55. Also, *Threave Gardens.*
Clatteringshaws Loch, nr New Galloway. *Galloway Deer Museum.* Live trout exhibition as well as features on deer, other aspects of wildlife, and geology and history in Galloway.
Creetown, nr Gatehouse of Fleet. *Cairnholy Chambered Cairns.* See page 55.
Creetown, nr Gatehouse of Fleet. *Gem/Rock Museum.* Rocks, minerals and semi-precious stones from all over the world.
Dumfries. *Burns' House.* Home of poet Robert Burns from 1793 to 1796.
Dumfries. *Dumfries Museum.* In a restored 18th century windmill. Has natural history, archaeology and folk collections, and a camera obscura.
Kirkcudbright. *Maclellan's Castle.* A ruined 16th century mansion, overlooking the harbour.
New Abbey, nr Dumfries. *Sweetheart Abbey.* See page 55.
Port Logan, nr Port Patrick. *Logan Botanic Gardens.* Gardens include cabbage palms, tree ferns and other plants from warm countries.
Shearington, nr Dumfries. *Caerlaverock Castle.* Triangular-shaped castle with round towers. Also, *Caerlaverock National Nature Reserve,* noted for wintering wildfowl.
Thornhill. *Drumlanrig Castle.* Built in 17th century in pink sandstone. Contains furniture and paintings. Adventure woodland and nature trail in parklands.
Wanlockhead, nr Sanquhar. *Museum of the Scottish Lead Mining Industry.* Includes a lead mine beam engine, a smelt and miners' cottages.
Wigtown. *Torhouse Stone Circle.* Probably dates from the Bronze Age.

FIFE (Map page 57)

Anstruther. *North Carr Lightship.* Now a floating museum with interior fitted out to show what life was like on board.
Anstruther. *Scottish Fisheries Museum.* Illustrates a Scottish fisherman's life. Includes a marine aquarium.
Arncroach, nr Anstruther. *Kellie Castle and Gardens.* Mainly 16th–17th century with plasterwork and painted panelling.
Ceres, nr Cupar. *Fife Folk Museum.* See page 56.
Culross, nr Dunfermline. *Culross Palace.* House with painted ceilings and walls.
Dunfermline. *Pittencrieff Park.* Has flower gardens, a glen, nature trails, an aviary, old steam engine, pets' corner and maze. Also *Pittencrieff House Museum,* with exhibits of local history and costumes.
Falkland. *Falkland Palace.* See page 57.
Lochty, nr Crail. *Lochty Private Railway.* 2½km long steam train rides.
Tentsmuir Point. *Tentsmuir Point National Nature Reserve.* Migrant birds. Nature trail.

GRAMPIAN (Map page 56)

Aberdeen. *James Dun's House.* A museum for children in house of former master of Aberdeen Grammar School.
Aberdeen. *Provost Skene's House.* 17th century furnished house with displays of local history and domestic life.
Alford. *Murray Park.* Nature trail and narrow gauge *Alford Valley Railway.*
Ballater. *Balmoral Castle.* One of the homes of the Queen. Grounds sometimes open when royal family not in residence.
Ballindaloch, nr Dufftown, *Glenfarclas Distillery.* See page 61.
Banchory. *Crathes Castle and Gardens.* 16th century baronial castle with painted ceilings. Nature trail.
Braemar. *Braemar Castle.* Turreted 17th century stronghold, built in an L-shape with a star-shaped curtain wall. Underground pit prison.
Dufftown. *Balvenie Castle.* 14th century moated castle.
Dufftown. *Glenfiddich and Balvenie Distilleries.* Demonstrations of how malt whisky is made.
Elgin. *Elgin Museum.* Includes fossils, prehistoric weapons, costumes and local domestic items.
Glen Tamar, nr Aboyne. *Braeloine Visitor Centre.* Nature trails and an exhibition about wildlife, farming and forestry in the area.
Kildrummy, nr Alford. *Kildrummy Castle.* Ruins of 13th century castle. Also *Kildrummy Castle Gardens.*
Kirkhill of Kennethmont, nr Huntly. *Leith Hall.* Contains military relics. Gardens have pond walk with an observation hide.
Muir of Fowlis, nr Alford. *Craigievar Castle.* See page 56.
Peterculter, nr Aberdeen. *Drum Castle.* 13th century tower adjoining 17th century mansion which contains furniture and silver. Grounds.
Peterhead. *Arbuthnot Museum.* Local history, whaling and an Arctic section.
Tarland, nr Ballater. *Culsh Earthworks.* See page 61.

HIGHLAND (Map pages 54, 58–59 and 60–61)

Alltnacaillich, nr Tongue. *Dun Dornadilla Broch.*
Aviemore. *Aviemore Centre.* A leisure and sports centre including a cinema, theatre, swimming pool, ice rink, artificial ski slope and go-karts. See also page 61.
Aviemore. *Aviemore Highland Craft Village.* Traditional village square where you can see craftsmen working on different arts and crafts.
Aviemore. *Clan Tartan Centre.* Films and exhibitions on history of clans and tartans.
Aviemore. *Santa Claus Land.* See page 30.
Ballachulish. *Glencoe and North Lorn Folk Museum.* Historic relics, domestic and farm implements, weapons, costumes and dolls.
Boat of Garten, nr Aviemore. *Strathspey Railway.* Steam train rides and museum.
Cannich, nr Inverness. *Corrimony Cairn.* Stone Age burial cairn with chamber.
Carrbridge, nr Grantown-on-Spey. *Landmark Visitor Centre.* Films and slides show history of Highlands from Ice Age on. Woodland nature trail.
Cawdor, nr Nairn. *Cawdor Castle.* See page 60.
Drumnadrochit. *Loch Ness Monster Museum.*
Dunbeath. *Laidhay Caithness Croft.* Croft with stable, house, byre and barn, furnished as it was in 18th century.
Dunvegan, Skye. *Dunvegan Castle.* See page 58. Boat trips from the castle to a seal colony.
Dunvegan, Skye. *Skye Watermill and Black House.* See page 58.
Durness. *Balnakeil Craft Village.* Craftsmen working at pottery, boatbuilding, etc.
Durness. *Smoo Cave.* Three huge caves in limestone cliffs, two of which you can go in.
Fort Augustus. *Great Glen Exhibition.* Tells the history of the Great Glen, including Loch Ness and the monster.
Fort William. *Neptune's Staircase.* A series of 8 locks on the Caledonian Canal.
Fort William. *West Highland Folk Museum.* Historical, natural history and folk exhibits.
Golspie, nr Dornoch. *Dunrobin Castle.* See page 60.
Handa Island. *Handa Island Nature Reserve.* A seabird sanctuary. Access by boat from Tarbet.
Inverness. *Clava Cairns.* A group of three prehistoric burial cairns and standing stones.
Inverness. *Culloden Moor.* Site of battle of Culloden, with clan graves, museum and visitor centre. See page 60.
Kincraig, nr Aviemore. *Highland Wildlife Park.* See page 31.
Kingussie. *Highland Folk Museum.* See page 61.
Kinlochewe. *Beinn Eighe National Nature Reserve.* Of geological and wildlife interest, with pine marten, wildcat, golden eagle, Arctic and Alpine plants. Nature trails and visitor centre.
Knockan, nr Ullapool. *Inverpolly National Nature Reserve.* Nature/geological trail and information centre.
Loch Garten, nr Aviemore. *Loch Garten Nature Reserve.* Ospreys and other wildlife.
Nairn. *Fishertown Museum.* Shows life of Nairn as prosperous fishing town in Victorian times.
Nairn. *Fort George.* See page 60. Also *Queen's Own Highlanders Museum* with medals and uniforms.
Reay, nr Thurso. *Dounreay Nuclear Power Establishment.* Exhibition about work being done at the establishment.
Torridon. *Torridon Visitor Centre.* Displays on wildlife. Nearby is *Torridon Deer Museum.*
Ullapool. *Highlands Museum.* History and natural life of region.
Wick. *Wick Heritage Centre.* Exhibition of domestic, fishing and farming life in the area.

LOTHIAN (Map page 57)

East Linton, nr Dunbar. *Preston Mill.* A working watermill.
Edinburgh. *Craigmillar Castle.* Ruins of huge fortress associated with Mary Queen of Scots.
Edinburgh. *Edinburgh Castle.* Built on a crag. Has great hall, armour, dungeons, state apartments, chapel, Scottish Crown Jewels and *Scottish National War Museum.*
Edinburgh. *Museum of Childhood.* Large collection of toys, books, dolls, dolls' houses, costumes and nursery equipment.
Edinburgh. *National Museum of Antiquities.* Collections show history and everyday life of

Scotland from Stone Age to modern times.
Edinburgh. *Outlook Tower and Camera Obscura.*
Edinburgh. *Palace of Holyroodhouse.* See page 57.
Edinburgh. *Philatelic Bureau.* Stamps and historic relics of postal services.
Edinburgh. *Royal Botanic Gardens.* See page 57.
Edinburgh. *Royal Scottish Museum.* Art and archaeology, natural history, geology, technology and science.
Edinburgh. *Scottish National Zoological Park.* See page 30.
Edinburgh. *The Georgian House.* At No. 7 Charlotte Square. Rooms furnished as they would have been in late 1700s.
Edinburgh. *Transport Museum.* Full-size and model exhibits of transport in city over the centuries.
Edinburgh. *Wax Museum.* Models of famous people from Scottish history, including a chamber of horrors.
Linlithgow. *Canal Museum.* History and wildlife of the Union Canal.
Linlithgow. *Linlithgow Palace.* Ruined palace on shore of loch. Birthplace of Mary Queen of Scots.
Linlithgow. *The House of the Binns.* 17th century house with fine plaster ceilings, panoramic viewpoint and visitor trail.
North Berwick. *Boat trips round Bass Rock.* See page 57.
North Berwick. *Museum of Flight.* Aircraft, aero-engines and rockets, including Blue Streak.
North Berwick. *Myreton Motor Museum.* Cars, commercial vehicles, motorcycles, bicycles and historic military vehicles.
Prestonpans. *Prestongrange Mining Museum and Historic Site.* On the site of an old colliery. Exhibits include an old beam pumping engine.
South Queensferry. *Hopetoun House.* See page 57.
Stenton, nr Dunbar. *Pressmennan Forest Trail.*
Torphichen, nr Bathgate. *Cairnpapple Hill.* Prehistoric stone circle and burial cairns.

ORKNEY ISLANDS (Map page 63)

Dounby, Mainland. *Click Mill.* A working watermill.
Finstown, Mainland. *Maes Howe.* Big prehistoric burial mound with passage and chamber and 12th century Viking inscriptions.
Kirkwall, Mainland. *Earl Patrick's Palace.* Built in 1607. Nearby is *Bishop's Palace,* built in 13th century with a 16th century round tower.
Kirkwall, Mainland. *Tankerness House.* A 16th century Orkney town house with courtyard and gardens, now a museum of life in Orkneys over past 4,000 years.
St Mary's, Mainland. *Italian Chapel.* Built by Italian prisoners in World War II out of scrap metal, etc.
Skaill, nr Stromness, Mainland. *Skara Brae.* A Stone Age village buried under sand dunes until excavation in 1850. You can see 7 small huts with stone beds, "cupboards" and hearths.
Stromness, Mainland. *Standing Stones of Stenness.* Remains of prehistoric stone circle.
Stromness, Mainland. *Stromness Museum.* Preserved birds, eggs and shells, and a maritime section including ship models.
Wyre, Isle of. *Cobbie Row's Castle.* Probably Scotland's oldest stone castle.

SHETLAND ISLANDS (Map page 63)

Lerwick, Mainland. *Shetland Museum.* Life in the Shetlands from prehistoric times to present day.
Sandwick, Mainland. *Mousa Broch.* Well-preserved Iron Age broch on an island off the mainland.
Sumburgh Head, Mainland. *Jarlshof.* See page 63.
Veensgarth, nr Lerwick, Mainland. *Tingwall Valley Agricultural Museum.* Tools and equipment used by Shetland crofters.

STRATHCLYDE (Map pages 54–55 and 59)

Auchindrain, nr Inverary. *Auchindrain Museum.* Furnished houses and barns showing life on a West Highland farm in 1800s.
Ayr. *Tam o' Shanter Museum.* A museum to do with poet Robert Burns.
Balloch, Loch Lomond. *Cameron Loch Lomond Wildlife and Leisure Park.* Drive-through reserves including bears. Boating, lochside picnic areas and gardens. Also *Cameron House,* which has an oriental room, nursery, collection of whisky bottles, and model aircraft.
Biggar. *Gladstone Court Museum.* See page 52.
Brodick, Arran. *Brodick Castle and Gardens.* See page 55.
Carsaig, Mull. *Carsaig Arches.* Tunnels made by the sea. Reached only at low tide by 5km walk.
Craignure, Mull. *Duart Castle.* See page 59.
Craignure, Mull. *Torosay Castle.* Victorian house in Scottish baronial style. Italian gardens.
Dervaig, Mull. *Old Byre Folk Museum.* Shows crofting life on Mull, using life-like figures and a sound commentary.
Glasgow. *Botanic Gardens.* Include tropical plants such as orchids and begonias and tree ferns.
Glasgow. *Calderpark Zoo.*
Glasgow. *Haggs Castle Museum.* See page 54.
Glasgow. *Museum of Transport.* See page 55.
Glasgow. *Pollok House.* Adam house with paintings, glass, furniture and pottery. Rhododendrons, woodlands and walks.
Glasgow. *Victoria Park and Fossil Grove.* Includes flower garden, arboretum and fossil tree stumps which are 230 million years old.
Great Cumbrae Island. *University Marine Biological Station.* Includes aquaria. Ferries sail from Largs.
Inchcailloch Island, Loch Lomond. *Loch Lomond National Nature Reserve.* Woodland and birds. Access by boat from Balmaha.
Inverary. *Inverary Castle.* See page 54.
Kilmartin, nr Lochgilphead. *Nether Largie Cairns.* Two Bronze Age and one Stone Age burial cairns.
Loch Scridain, Mull. *The Burg.* A fossil tree. Reached by 8km walk on north shore of loch only at low tide.
Maybole. *Culzean Country Park.* Includes an aviary, swan pond and orangery. Also *Culzean Castle.* See page 55.
Maybole. *Kilkerran Farm.* Off B741 south of Maybole. A modern working farm which you can visit. There are pony and trailer rides.
Maybole. *Moorston Farm.* Off B741 south of Maybole. Modern farm where you can see cattle and various types of farm machinery.
Rothesay, Bute. *Rothesay Castle.* Medieval castle with circular courtyard.
Staffa, off Mull. *Fingal's Cave.* Huge cave with weird basalt rock formataions. Seen by boat trips from Oban or Mull.
Uddingston, nr Glasgow. *Bothwell Castle.* Remains of 13th century stone castle.

TAYSIDE (Map pages 54 and 56–57)

Aberfeldy. *Castle Menzies.* 16th century fortified tower house with turrets, built in shape of letter Z.
Arbroath. *St Vigean's Museum.* A cottage museum with gravestones from time of the Picts.
Auchterarder, nr Crieff. *Strathallan Air Museum.* Historic aircraft.
Ben Lawers, nr Loch Tay. *Ben Lawers Visitor Centre.* Tells the story of the mountain. There is also a nature trail.
Blair Atholl, nr Pitlochry. *Blair Castle.* See page 56.
Braco, nr Crief. *Ardoch Roman Camp.* Remains of a Roman fort.
Comrie. *Museum of Scottish Tartans.* See page 54.
Dundee. *Broughty Castle Museum.* Whaling relics, including harpoons, knives, axes, boat models and carved ivory and shells.
Dundee. *Camperdown Park Wildlife Centre.* Animals and birds, wildlife ponds, woodland nature trails and an information centre.
Dundee. *Frigate Unicorn.* See page 56.
Dundee. *Mills Observatory.* An astronomical observatory with telescopes you can use and a small planetarium.
Glamis, nr Forfar. *Angus Folk Museum.* Relics of domestic and agricultural life in 1800s and before.
Glamis, nr Forfar. *Glamis Castle.* Historic castle, redesigned in 17th century in style of a French château. Has collections of china, tapestry and furniture and grounds by Capability Brown. See also page 56.
Kinross. *Loch Leven Castle.* On island in loch. Access by ferry.
Kinross. *Vane Farm Nature Reserve.* On south shore of Loch Leven. Many wild geese and ducks in winter. Nature centre has displays about the loch and surrounding countryside. Nature trail.
Perth. *Balboughty Farm.* Working farm where you can see cattle, sheep, crops and machinery.
Perth. *Scone Palace.* Largely rebuilt in 1803, contains furniture, china, ivories, clocks, vases and needlework. Woodland gardens.
Pitlochry. *Pitlochry Power Station and Dam.* There is an exhibition about hydro-electric power in the power station and you can see salmon in a fish ladder.

WESTERN ISLES (Map pages 58–59)

Arnol, Lewis. *Lewis Black House.* A traditional type of house in the Western Isles, furnished and with a byre inside.
Callanish, Lewis. *Callanish Standing Stones.* See page 58.
Carloway, Lewis. *Dun Carloway Broch.* Remains of an Iron Age broch.
Loch Druidibeg, South Uist. *Loch Druidibeg National Nature Reserve.* See page 59.
Shawbost, Lewis. *Shawbost Folk Museum.* There is a restored Scandinavian watermill nearby.

NORTHERN IRELAND

CO. ANTRIM (Map pages 62–63)

Aghagallon, S.E. Lough Neagh. *"The Willow Pattern Garden".* A folly garden built with queer shaped stones, including fossils and petrified wood from Lough Neagh.
Antrim. *Antrim Castle Park.* 17th century gardens, including a ruined castle.
Antrim. *The Round Tower.* Remains of a monastery, built in the 9th century.
Antrim. *Shanes Castle.* See page 63.
Ballintoy. *Carrick-a-rede Rope Bridge.* A narrow bridge made of planks with wire handrails, 25m above the sea to an offshore island.
Belfast. *City of Belfast Zoo.*
Belfast. *Transport Museum.* Includes steam engines and railway carriages, trams, horse coaches, carriages, vans, cars and motorbikes.
Belfast. *Ulster Museum Botanic Gardens.* Displays on the landscape and natural history of Northern Ireland. Also visit the *Palm House.*
Bellahill, nr Whitehead. *Dalway's Bawn.* 17th century fortified farmhouse.
Benvarden, nr Coleraine. *Causeway Coast Safari Park.* Includes lions. Also has a children's zoo, miniature railway and "space travel" hall.
Bushmills. *The Giant's Causeway.* See page 62.
Carrickfergus. *Carrickfergus Castle.* See page 63.
Glenarm. *Glenarm Castle.* 17th century castle with later additions.
Holywood, nr Belfast. *Ulster Folk and Transport Museum, Cultra Manor.* See page 63.
Portrush. *The White Rocks.* Chalk cliffs between Portrush and Dunluce Castle, full of interesting caves and rock formations.
Rathlin Island. Reached by motorboat from Ballycastle. A good place for birdwatching.
Whitehead. *Railway Preservation Society of Ireland.* Runs various steam train rides.

CO. ARMAGH (Map page 62)

Armagh. *The Planetarium.* See page 62.
Armagh. *The County Museum.*
Armagh. *Navan Fort.* See page 62.
Bessbrook. *Derrymore House.* Late 18th century thatched manor house.
Portadown. *Ardress House.* 17th century house with plasterwork and pictures. There is a farm museum and wooded grounds.

CO. DOWN (Map page 63)

Ballylesson. *The Giant's Ring.* Huge Stone Age earthwork, with "The Druid's Altar" dolmen in the middle.
Ballynahinch. *Harris's Mill.* Old corn mill with a working waterwheel.
Bangor. *Ward Park.* Includes ponds with waterfowl, nature trail and children's zoo.
Downpatrick. *Ballynoe Stone Circle.*
Greencastle, Carlingford Lough. *Greencastle.* Ruins of a large 13th century Norman castle.

Killyleagh, Strangford Lough. *Killyleagh Castle.* Built in the 12th century, but much altered.
Millisle, nr Donaghadee. *Ballycopeland Windmill.* See page 63. Nearby at Killaughey is a blacksmith's forge.
Newcastle. *Dundrum Castle.* Ruins of a large Norman castle.
Newtownards. *Mount Stewart.* House designed by Robert Adam. Garden includes rare plants and shrubs, topiary and a statuary with figures of dodos, dinosaurs, griffins, etc.
Saintfield. *Rowallane Gardens.*
Strangford. *Castle Ward.* See page 63.
Warrenpoint. *Narrow Water Castle.* 16th century 3-storey tower built to defend the estuary.

CO. FERMANAGH (Map page 62)

Belleek. *Belleek Pottery.* See page 62.
Belleek. *Castle Caldwell.* Nature reserve and a ruined castle.
Devenish Island, Lower Lough Erne. *Devenish Round Tower.* 12th century round tower and the remains of a monastery. You can reach the island by ferry.
Enniskillen. *Castlecoole.* 18th century mansion. Contains furnishings and paintings.
Enniskillen. *Enniskillen Castle.*
Enniskillen. *Florence Court.* 18th century house containing fine plasterwork and furniture.
Linasken. *Castle Balfour.* 17th century castle.
Monea. *Monea Castle.* Ruined castle.

CO. LONDONDERRY (Map page 62)

Downhill–Magilligan Point. *Magilligan Strand.* Ireland's longest beach, which has lots of different kinds of shells.
Drumsurn. *Kings Fort.* Prehistoric rath (mound) with a deep moat.
Limavady. *Roe Valley Country Park.* Riverside walks with interesting wildlife. Also Ulster's first hydro-electric power station and some old watermills.
Londonderry. *Londonderry City Walls.* Built in the 17th century, these are the only unbroken walls around any British city.
Moneymore. *Springhill House.* 17th century house with interesting library and collection of curios, a costume museum and a kitchen.

CO. TYRONE (Map page 62)

Augher. *Knockmany Forest and Chambered Cairn.* The forest is in the Sperrin Mountains, and includes an interesting prehistoric cairn.
Caledon. *Caledon Castle.* Georgian house with interior plasterwork by Adam, and fine paintings. Deer park.
Camphill, nr Omagh. *Ulster American Folk Park.* See page 62.
Cookstown. *Beaghmore Stone Circle.*
Dungannon. *Tyrone Crystal.* You can take a tour round the glass factory.
Kildress, nr Cookstown. *Wellbrook Beetling Mill.* 18th century water-powered mill, with great wheel and sluices in working order.
Newtownstewart. *Baronscourt Forest and Deer Centre.* Includes wildlife and nature exhibition and a nature trail.
Newtownstewart. *Killeter Forest.* Riverside nature trail and red deer.
Omagh. *Seskinore Forest.* Walks, wildlife and many different birds.
Strabane. *Grey's Printing Shop.* 18th century shop which contains old printing presses.

Map Index

General Index

Useful Addresses

National tourist boards

The national or regional tourist boards listed below will be able to give you the addresses of the many local tourist information offices throughout Britain.

British Tourist Authority, 64 St James's St, London SW1A 1NF. Tel: (01) 499 9325.
English Tourist Board, 4 Grosvenor Gardens, London SW1W 0DU.
Wales Tourist Board, 3 Castle St, Cardiff CF1 2RE. Tel: Cardiff 27281.
Scottish Tourist Board, 23 Ravelston Terrace, Edinburgh EH4 3EU. Tel: (031) 332 2433.
Scottish Tourist Board, 5 Pall Mall East, London SW1. Tel: (01) 930 8661.
Northern Ireland Tourist Board, River House, 48 High St, Belfast BT1 2DS. Tel: Belfast 31221.
Northern Ireland Tourist Board, c/o Ulster Office, 11 Berkeley St, London W1X 6BU. Tel: (01) 493 0601.

Regional tourist boards

IN ENGLAND

Cumbria Tourist Board, Ellerthwaite, Windermere, Cumbria LA23 2AQ.
East Anglia Tourist Board, (counties: Cambs., Essex, Norfolk and Suffolk), 14 Museum St, Ipswich, Suffolk IP1 1HU. Tel: Ipswich 214211.
East Midlands Tourist Board, (counties: Derby., Leics., Lincs., Northants. and Notts.), Exchequergate, Lincoln LN1 3AR. Tel: Lincoln 31521.
Heart of England Tourist Board, (counties: Glos., Heref. and Worcs., Shropshire, Staffs., Warks. and W. Midlands), PO Box 15, Worcs. WR1 2JT. Tel: Worcs. 29511.
Isle of Man Tourist Board, 13 Victoria St, Douglas, Isle of Man. Tel: Douglas 4323.
Isle of Wight Tourist Board, 21 High St, Newport, Isle of Wight PO30 1JS. Tel: Newport 524343.
London Tourist Board, 26 Grosvenor Gardens, London SW1W 0DU. Tel: (01) 730 0791.
Northumbria Tourist Board, (counties: Cleveland, Durham, Northumberland, Tyne and Wear), 9 Osborne Terrace, Newcastle upon Tyne NE2 1NT. Tel: Newcastle 817744.
North West Tourist Board, (counties: Cheshire, Derby. (High Peak only), Gtr Manchester, Lancs. and Mers.), The Last Drop Village, Bromley Cross, Bolton BL7 9PZ. Tel: Bolton 591511.
South East England Tourist Board, (counties: E. Sussex, Kent, Surrey and W. Sussex), Cheviot House, 4–6 Monson Rd, Tunbridge Wells, Kent TN1 1NH. Tel: Tunbridge Wells 40766.
Southern Tourist Board, (counties: parts of Dorset, Hants. and I. of Wight), Old Town Hall, Leigh Rd, Eastleigh, Hants. SO5 4DE. Tel: Eastleigh 616027.
Thames and Chilterns Tourist Board, (counties: Beds., Berks., Bucks., Herts. and Oxfordshire), PO Box 10, 8 The Market Place, Abingdon, Oxfordshire OX14 3UD. Tel: Abingdon 22711.
West Country Tourist Board, (counties: Avon, Cornwall, Devon, parts of Dorset, Somerset, Wilts. and Scilly Isles), Trinity Court, 37 Southernhay East, Exeter, Devon EX1 1QS. Tel: Exeter 76351.
Yorkshire and Humberside Tourist Board, (counties: Humberside, N., S. and W. Yorks.), 312 Tadcaster Rd, York YO2 2HF. Tel: York 707961.

IN WALES

Mid Wales Tourism Council, (counties: parts of Dyfed, Gwynedd and Powys), The Owain Glyndwr Centre, Machynlleth, Powys. Tel: Machynlleth 2401.
North Wales Tourism Council, (counties: Clwyd, most of Gwynedd), Civic Centre, Colwyn Bay, Clwyd LL29 8 AR. Tel: Colwyn Bay 56881.
South Wales Tourism Council, (counties: parts of Dyfed and Powys, Gwent, Mid, South and W. Glam.), Darkgate, Carmarthen, Dyfed. Tel: Carmarthen 7557.

IN SCOTLAND

Borders Regional Council, Tourism Division, Regional Headquarters, Newtown St Boswells TD6 0SA. Tel: St Boswells 3301.
Central Regional Council, Tourism Department (E), Viewforth, Stirling FK8 2ET. Tel: Stirling 3111.
Dumfries and Galloway Tourist Association, Douglas House, Newton Stewart DG8 6ED. Tel: Newton Stewart 2549.
Fife Tourist Authority, Fife House, North St, Glenrothes KY7 5LT. Tel: Glenrothes 754411.
Grampian Regional Council, Leisure, Recreation and Tourism Department, Woodhill House, Ashgrove Rd West, Aberdeen AB9 2LU. Tel: Aberdeen 682222.
Highlands and Islands Tourism Council, Information Office, 54 High St, Grantown-on-Spey.
Lothian Regional Council, Department of Leisure Services, 40 Torphichen St, Edinburgh EH3 8JJ.
Orkney Tourist Organization, Broad St, Kirkwall, Orkneys. Tel: Kirkwall 2856.
Shetland Tourist Organization, Alexander Wharf, The Esplanade, Lerwick, Shetlands. Tel: Lerwick 3434.
Strathclyde Regional Council, Department of Leisure and Recreation, McIver House, Cadogan St, Glasgow G2 7QB. Tel: (041) 204 2900.
Tayside Regional Council, Department of Recreation and Tourism, Tayside House, 26–28 Crichton St, Dundee DD1 3RD.
Western Isles Tourism Organization, 4 South Beach St, Stornoway, Western Isles. Tel: Stornoway 3088.

Some other organizations mentioned in this book

Countryside Commission, John Dower House, Crescent Place, Cheltenham, Glos. GL50 3RA.
Countryside Commission for Scotland, Battleby, Redgorton, Perth PH1 3EW.
Brecon Beacons National Park, Glamorgan St, Brecon, Powys LD3 7DP.
Dartmoor National Park, "Parke", Haytor Rd, Bovey Tracey, Devon TQ13 9JQ.
Exmoor National Park, Exmoor House, Dulverton, Somerset TA22 9HL.
Lake District National Park, Bank House, High St, Windermere, Cumbria LA23 1AF.
North York Moors National Park, The Old Vicarage, Bondgate, Helmsley, N. Yorks. YO6 5BP.
Northumberland National Park, Eastburn, South Park, Hexham, N'land NE46 1BS.
Peak District National Park, Aldern House, Baslow Rd, Bakewell, Derby. DE4 1AE.
Pembrokeshire Coast National Park, County Offices, Haverfordwest, Dyfed SA61 1QZ.
Snowdonia National Park, Yr Hen Ysgol, Maentwrog, Blaenau Ffestiniog, Gwynedd LL41 4HW.
Yorkshire Dales National Park, Colvend, Hebden Rd, Grassington, Skipton, N. Yorks. BD23 5LB.
Forestry Commission, 231 Corstorphine Rd, Edinburgh EH12 7AT.
Department of Agriculture (Northern Ireland), Forest Service, Dundonald House, Upper Newtownards Rd, Belfast BT4 3SB.
Department of the Environment (Northern Ireland), Conservation Branch, Stormont, Belfast BT4 3SS.
National Trust, 42 Queen Anne's Gate, London SW1H 9AS.
National Trust for Scotland, 5 Charlotte Sq., Edinburgh EH2 4DU.
National Trust for Northern Ireland, Rowallane House, Saintfield, Ballynahinch, Co. Down BT24 7LH.
Nature Conservancy Council, 19–20 Belgrave Sq., London SW1X 8PY.
Nature Conservancy Council for Wales, Ffondd Penrhos, Bangor, Gwynedd LL57 2LQ.
Nature Conservancy Council for Scotland, 12 Hope Terrace, Edinburgh EH9 2AS.
Water Space Amenity Commission, 1 Queen Anne's Gate, London SW1H 9BT.
Wildfowl Trust, Slimbridge, Glos. GL2 7BT.
Watch Club, Society for the Promotion of Nature Conservation, The Green, Nettleham, Lincoln LN2 2NR.
Wildlife Youth Service, World Wildlife Fund, Wallington, Surrey SM6 0DN.
British Naturalists' Association, 2a London Rd, Thatcham, Berks. RG13 4LP.
British Trust for Conservation Volunteers, 10–14 Duke St, Reading, Berks. RG1 4RU.
Field Studies Council, Preston Montford, Montford Bridge, Shrewsbury, Shropshire SY4 1HW.
Young Ornithologists' Club, Royal Society for the Protection of Birds, The Lodge, Sandy, Beds. SG19 2DL.
British Trust for Ornithology, Beech Grove, Tring, Herts.